THIS BOOK IS DEDICATED TO EILEEN, PETER AND DOROTHY.
MAY ALL BEINGS BE WELL AND HAPPY.

FINDHORN FLOWER ESSENCES
HANDBOOK

Marion Leigh

NATURE SPIRITS PUBLISHING

ISBN: 978-0-9574196-0-5

Cullerne House
Findhorn
Morayshire
Scotland
IV36 3YY

info@findhornessences.com
www.findhornessences.com

Acknowledgements

THE AUTHOR AND PUBLISHERS
WOULD LIKE TO THANK THE FOLLOWING:

DOROTHY MACLEAN for her Foreword, her generosity and inspiration

SUSAN KEMP for her fine editing and proofing

LILA SIMITZI (Greece) for her love and passion through design

WHITE DESIGN (Greece) for the book concept, design and layout

ADRIAN for project management with dedication and aplomb

IONA, my loving daughter, for the illustrations of flowers, *chakras,* elements, rays
and zodiac illustrations for the flower attunement cards and much more

SUKANYA CARAGH MCAULEY for botanical illustrations for the original book

GWYNETH for her helpful, very critical editing

CHRISTINE AND ELISABETH, angels of production

DAVID for the glossary, editing and esoteric intelligence

ROB for unconditional love and support

MICHAEL AND GAVIN – thanks for the laughs!

Contents

Foreword

All of nature is a doorway to the divine, and the beauty of flowers - their colours, their scents, their shapes, even their feel - continually amaze us, delight our senses and open our hearts. Somehow they speak to us on all levels, and reach into our essence.

Each one of us reacts differently to flowers. Nowadays people all over the world are recognising that flowers can not only delight us, but touch us deeply enough to change us. Perhaps change is the wrong word, for what they do, as we open ourselves to their beauty is to awaken in us the same qualities that they embody. Their beauty is obvious. Ours is often hidden. At this time, methods for making their essence available to us in a material form have been discovered.

Marion Leigh is one who is very open to the essence of flowers. Here she tells of her experience in connecting deeply with nature and how she was guided to make flower essences. Her story is naturally unique, for we are all unique beings. She shares how her story unfolds and how she was guided to continue to explore nature according to her own inner nature. As in all stories that tell of the wonderful world of nature, which is always talking to us if we would just listen, we are helped to connect with and recognise our own participation in the environment, in the world, and we are helped to trust the workings of the universe. Stories of inner attunement confirm our links with all life, and above all, can help us to live our everyday life in the best way we know. The deeper our connections with everything around us, the more we appreciate life and its joys.

The quality most necessary for deep contact with anything is love. As we explore life, as we explore flowers, as we accept varying circumstances, as we grow, we realise more and more the power of love. So our love grows, and we become our own essence, which is love. Flower essences cannot but help us to this realization.

DOROTHY MACLEAN

Introduction

I began making flower essences at Findhorn in 1992. I did not set out to start a line of essences. On arriving back here from Australia, having just left working with Ian White and the Australian Bush Flower Essences, it followed that I would continue working with ABFE in Europe. The Findhorn Flower Essences grew organically from a personal need for remedies to help me make the adjustment of uprooting my family and moving to the other side of the world, and the incredible upheaval that followed. Making essences from my immediate environment was simply led by my common sense. Not until doing Dorothy Maclean's workshop towards the end of that first year did the 'penny drop'. Dorothy told me she always knew flower essences would be made at Findhorn but that this had not been up to her. "Why not you?" she asked me.

By then there were a dozen essences, the thirteenth followed in February 1993. Making Snowdrop coincided with Peter Caddy's death (it's helpful for grief). This is an example of how a number of the flower essences were spontaneously developed, the timing of making them corresponding with a need, and guided by intuition.

Over the succeeding twenty years the range expanded to forty-eight flowers, seven elemental and environmental essences, seven gem essences and 28 combination formulas for common shared life issues.

This handbook follows on from my first book published in 1997, long out of print. This edition is a comprehensive guide to the all the essences, with instructions in their use. The index at the back is a repertoire of emotional indications and will guide the seeker of a flower essence to a listing of remedies that may be helpful, as well as directing you to further 'keywords' of possible concomitant indications to pursue.

Essences are created in accordance with three forces: cosmic, natural and human. The cosmic forces are harnessed using the energies available at any specific time: the zodiacal influences, the full and new moons, the time of day (movement of etheric energies in building up and releasing). The natural forces relate to the 'power points' or *chakras* on the landscape. The human element is the heart attuned to all the above and in co-creation with the energies and intelligence in nature.

MARION LEIGH

Good Vibrations

Flower essences are aqueous infusions of flowers, endowed with the very essence and the highest concentration of the life force of a plant. The etheric energies of the flowers are transferred into pure water and the resulting infusion, the 'mother essence', is preserved with brandy and then becomes the 'mother tincture'. They are classified as vibrational medicine, the healing vibratory 'signature' of the flower corresponding with an emotion or state of mind, and are used to treat the emotional, mental and spiritual nature rather than the physical body.

The premise of treating the causes of illness has been recognised since the time of Hippocrates, the 'Father of Medicine'. The role of flower essences is to assist in clearing the emotional or astral body of those conditions that predispose people to disease.

Findhorn Flower Essences are made by the sun infusion method pioneered in the 1930s by Dr Edward Bach, an eminent Harley Street physician, homeopathic practitioner and sensitive. Long before Dr Bach's legacy of the 38 Healers, Paracelsus (1493-1541), the Swiss Renaissance physician, botanist and alchemist, wrote of collecting dew from blossoms to treat emotional imbalances. Evidence exists for the use of flowers for healing in ancient Egypt, by the Celtic Druids, and by Aboriginal people around the world. It is therefore probable that flower essences have been around since time immemorial.

THE MIND-BODY CONNECTION

Our human existence is becoming increasingly artificial and more stressful. Stress is recognised as a major cause of unhappiness, frequently leading us down the slippery slope to physical illness. Unfortunately, orthodox medicines such as tranquillisers will not free our minds and bodies from stress although they may ease our discomfort by dulling our perceptions and reactions to stress.

Flower essences work on the subtle levels of our human anatomy. They work in our 'energy bodies' and we experience them energetically. Machaelle Wright of the Perelandra Centre for Nature Research claims that flower essences "repair, balance and stabilise the human electrical system", which then stabilises the nervous system, thereby halting the domino effect that leads to physical illness.

There are very few instruments that are able to measure the effect of flower and vibrational essences on the subtle levels of the human anatomy, the etheric body and the *chakras,* and the astral or emotional body. Homeopathy, which has been in use for two hundred years, also cannot be scientifically proven. Recent research into the 'memory of water' may give one explanation as to how essences and homeopathic remedies work. Water is a carrier of energy and can be imprinted with energy by contact with a physical substance, or by conscious human intent.

Masaru Emoto, the well-known researcher into the memory of water, says: "If water collects information and its crystals reflect those characteristics, it means that the quality of water changes based on the information it receives. In other words, the information we give to water changes its quality." Water makes up between seventy and eighty percent of the bodies of all living things and is the most important solvent known, having the ability to assimilate the properties of other things. Researchers in Russia found that when a magnet is kept in contact with water over a period of time, the water becomes magnetically charged. Their studies showed that magnetised water has positive effects on the human body when taken internally, although they admitted to the world that their scientists were not able to give an explanation as to why water changed when exposed to magnetic fields. The Russians began using magnetised water in their hospitals many years ago.

However, scientists around the world continue to dismiss the Russian discoveries and the hypothesis that water can retain memory of a substance that it no longer contains.

Dr Bach, who said that health depends on being in harmony with our souls, explains the action of essences thus: "To raise our vibrations and open up our channels for the reception of our spiritual self, to flood our natures with the particular virtues and to wash out from us the faults which were causing them, they are able, like beautiful music or any gloriously uplifting thing which gives us inspiration, to raise our very natures and bring us nearer to ourselves and by that very act to bring us peace and relieve our suffering. They cure not by attacking disease but by flooding our bodies with beautiful vibrations of our higher nature in the presence of which disease melts as snow in the sunshine."
Bach, E. (1931), Ye Suffer from Yourselves by Dr E Bach from lecture given in Southport, 1931

Dr Richard Gerber, author of the groundbreaking book *Vibrational Medicine for the 21st Century* says, "Our physical bodies are controlled by many biochemical cellular systems which are, in turn, finely tuned by subtle energy systems including the acupuncture meridian system and the *chakra* system. While our physical body is nurtured by physical nutrients and oxygen, it is also fed by subtle environmental energies such as chi and *prana,* which we absorb through the meridian and *chakra* networks. These subtle energetic forms of nutrition, understood by the ancients of China and India, are just as important as food and water to sustaining life. The subtle energy networks also connect the physical body to another type of energy system- the energy body- which is a holographic energy template that invisibly guides human growth and development. Modern technology has begun to validate ancient wisdom in a marriage of science and spirituality the like of which has not been seen on this planet for thousands of years. It is only through a fuller appreciation of a multidimensional model of human functioning that subtle energy therapies, such as flower essences, can be truly understood. [...]It is only when one takes into account the larger picture of human beings from a newly evolving multidimensional perspective that flower essences as a healing modality begin to make sense. Flower essences modify energy flow through the acupuncture meridians, the *chakras* and the subtle bodies with the end result of affecting the very energetic patterns that influence consciousness."

Magic in the Garden

"TO ATTUNE TO THE FLOWERS YOU MUST BE IN CONSCIOUS CONTACT WITH YOUR OWN SOUL OR DIVINE PRESENCE. THROUGH THIS ATTUNEMENT ONE CAN BECOME AWARE OF THE ONENESS OF CONSCIOUSNESS, OF LOVE, BEHIND AND IN THE WHOLE OF CREATION AND THEN THROUGH THIS YOU CAN ENTER INTO CONTACT WITH FLOWERS AND KNOW THE EXPRESSION OF THE DIVINE IN THE FLOWER, THE UNDERLYING ASPIRATION OF THE FLOWERS FOR THE DIVINE. LOVE OF FLOWERS BRINGS YOU INTO THE EXPERIENCE OF LOVE WITHIN THE SELF AND WHEN YOU ARE PERCEPTIVE TO THE INNER EXPRESSION WITHIN AND BETWEEN YOU, PERHAPS THROUGH THE BEAUTY OF FLOWERS, IT CAN LEAD TO AN AWAKENING BY NATURE WITHIN YOU TO THE CONSCIOUSNESS UNDERLYING THE MANIFESTED FORM."

THE MOTHER

A question I am frequently asked is how the essences developed at Findhorn differ from other lines, for example, the Bach remedies. There is no short answer to this. To explain, I have to go back to the beginning, to the place from where the essences emerge...

The magic in the gardens of the Findhorn Foundation is world-renowned and the community that has grown up over the past fifty years has promulgated the principles and practice of attunement to, and cooperation with, the kingdoms of nature. It is the expression and manifestation of its founders and those who have been guided to follow in their footsteps; attunement to the divine spirit within us and within all nature around us. From this awareness the garden at Findhorn grew and flourished. It has nourished the minds, bodies and spirits of the people drawn here, and this conscious cooperation with nature within and without was the first principle in working in these gardens.

In The Findhorn Garden, Professor R Lindsay Robb of the Soil Association speaks about the vitality and vibrancy of the gardens,
"The vigour, health and bloom of the plants in this garden at mid-winter on land which is almost barren, powdery sand cannot be explained by the moderate dressings of compost, nor indeed by the application of any known cultural methods of organic husbandry. There are other factors and they are vital ones."

Dubbed "Factor X" by the Soil Association, the "other factor" was conscious co-operation with nature.

The following descriptions on the process of attunement by their very necessity fall outside the realms of empirical science. Conventional science and rational thought, while having their place, have definite limits when it comes to an explanation of the entire myriad of energies, forces and beings that make up our environment. Science does not have the instruments to measure the vibrational frequency of flower essences let alone other universal phenomena. When science cannot measure and analyse it loudly declares that "it does not exist". At one time the most learned bodies declared the Earth was flat and the centre of the Universe!

The ability to communicate and connect with the over-lighting intelligences in nature is innate. Our task is to make it conscious. When, in our hearts and minds and in the spirit of love, we bridge the seeming separation between the unseen spiritual worlds and us, we find joyful oneness with nature, and the power to co-create with it.

ATTUNEMENT

The process or practice of attunement is explained thus by David Spangler, founder of the Findhorn Foundation's educational programme, "We begin with understanding the concept of oneness, that there is no real separation and that everything exists within a unified field of being.

The revealed nature of the oneness of creation is unfolding for us a dramatic and natural technique for transcending our human level of consciousness and communicating directly with vaster dimensions of being. We call this technique attunement.

To communicate with a level of Life apparently outside us, we simply discover and attune to its corresponding reality within us. We realise there is no separation, that essentially we are one with that level and we accept that oneness as the reality.

With the practice of attunement, we find ourselves in increasing communication with higher and vaster realms of Life, both vertically in terms of higher frequency consciousness and horizontally in terms of physical life that surrounds us as fellow human beings and the lives within nature.

Attunement is communication through communion, through recognising the wealth of oneness that has always been there. Unlike old-style communication, which is seen as a flow between two or more centres or people and thereby maintaining the concept of separation, in attunement there is no flow between, there is oneness with."

VITAL BEINGS

In my own practice of attunement I consciously recognise the presences of the elemental energies in nature. According to early traditions, and from Alchemy, these are the spirit beings of earth, air, fire and water. They are the builders of form, following the blueprint held by the *devas,* the 'architects' of form. Learning to work with them is a dynamic way of attuning to all of the energies of nature and their effects upon us. It facilitates 'mastery' over our own energy systems on all levels. Hence the alchemical process of turning lead into gold is a symbol of transmuting and transforming leaden-like consciousness into golden light consciousness.

Elemental energies fuel us with the vital energies we need to feel alive. Each elemental being reflects a basic energy pattern as it builds and manifests in nature. These interweave to create and sustain all matter on earth. It is said that in working with us the elemental beings are able to move higher within the hierarchy of life.

My awareness of the elementals was heightened when I was directed to make essences embodying the archetypal elemental energies. Sitting by the Findhorn River one sunny day in the summer of 1993, I was mesmerised by the power of the flowing water and, without a second thought, took out my glass bowl to prepare an essence. I felt the power of the river, a symbol of the very lifeblood, feeding and nourishing this landscape from its source in the Monadhliath mountains, to the Findhorn estuary.

The spirits of the earth are sometimes referred to as 'gnomes' and they are the fosterers of life. As Rudolf Steiner says, they, with the help of the fire spirits, "instill life into the plant and push it upwards. They carry the life ether to the root, the same life ether in which they live."

For gnomes the solid earth is hollow and offers no resistance. Gnomes transform the spirit currents flowing downward from the blossom and fruit into the roots and carry the ideas of the whole universe streaming throughout the world.

Water spirits are known as 'undines' and also 'nymphs'. Without water there would be no life and the spirits of water bring replenishment. Our ancestors regarded water as a living creature with the power to bestow the life force, health and energy. The undines symbolise abundant energy. In man they maintain the astral body, the flowing streams of the body and stimulate the feeling nature. Working with them can assist us in controlling and directing dream activity and to feel the fullest ecstasy of the creative acts of life. In the plant world, Rudolf Steiner says the undines work with the leaves, "In their dreaming they bind and release in their weavings the substances of the air which they mysteriously introduce into the leaves. They are the world chemists."

Air spirits or 'sylphs' bring inspiration and creativity. Many work for the creation of air and the atmospheric currents. In the human being they maintain the mental body, help stimulate new knowledge and inspiration and assist in using intuitive and rational thinking together. Through breath and air we assimilate power. The true power of the word is awakened with the aid of the spirits of air and they are critical to the development of clairaudience and telepathy. The energy is stimulating, changeable and can awaken greater intellect and strength of will. Steiner says the sylphs "live in the air warmth element...press toward the light; relate themselves to it - to the vibrations in a body of air. This spiritually sounding moving element of air. They absorb what the power of light sends into these vibrations of the air..... the cosmic bearers of love through the atmosphere, the bearers of wishes of love through the universe.

In the plant their task is to bear light into the plant. The power of the sylphs in the plant works on the chemical forces that were induced into the plant by the undines. Here occurs the interworking of sylph-light and undine chemistry. The sylphs weave out of the light the ideal plant form."

The elementals of fire are called 'salamanders' and bring stimulating, radiant vitality. Fire spirits hold the keys to the processes of alchemy as agents of transmutation, transformation and regeneration. The fiery element is both constructive and destructive, assisting in destroying the old and building the new and so very effective in healing work, helping to develop catalytic healing energies. Their energies are very stirring; their effect vitalising and can stimulate strong emotional currents and passions, sometimes difficult to control and direct. For this reason, the best method of control is through tranquil, placid contentment where they will instill great inspiration and spiritual idealism and perception. The fire spirits are enticed by music and strong rhythms. In plants, Steiner says, "they are the inhabitants of the warmth-light element. When warmth of earth is at its height or otherwise suitable, they gather the warmth together, ...carry it to the blossoms of the plants, ...carry the warmth into the seed, ...carry concentrated cosmic warmth on the little airships of anther-pollens".

SHINING ONES
Guiding and directing the work of the elemental beings stand the angels, or devas. (The word 'deva' comes from the Sanskrit and means 'shining one'.) According to Dorothy Maclean, devas are archetypal thoughts or energies. The idea that there are such beings is not new, and much of the world's literature down through the ages is full of myths, legends, fairy-tales and allegories relating to the shining ones.
People who are close to nature, artistic and sensitive seem most able to contact the deva kingdom, particularly in parts of the world where there are mountains, seas, lakes and where there are beauty spots almost 'magical' in their atmosphere.
My understanding of the deva-angel-man relationship is that we belong to a composite body and work together to fulfill the purposes of natural law and human evolution. From the smallest to the highest, each entity being has its own particular work to perform and as the most exalted angel uses his mighty intelligence in the forming of worlds, so the tiny nature spirit uses his powers in directing the processes of the plant kingdom. It is by coming into closer contact that we will come more and more into oneness with the spirit of Nature itself, and to understand the depths of her beauty. The unfolding of conscious relating between the two kingdoms, angelic and human, will facilitate a learning from and helping of the other. For all life, whether visible or invisible, is subject to this one evolutionary law, and each part must work together to carry out fully the divine will.
In unfolding our collective purpose through conscious contact and communication with the deva or angelic realm, humanity may discover its true place in the scheme of things.

These quotes from various works of Alice Bailey elaborate on my own thoughts on devas.

"THE DEVAS ARE THE ORIGIN OF FORM, THE VEHICLE OF DIVINE THOUGHT. THEY ARE THE SUM TOTAL OF THE SUBSTANCE OF THE SEVEN PLANES OF OUR SOLAR SYSTEM. A GREAT DEVA LORD RULES EACH PLANE. THE PLANE IS HIS BODY, THEY ARE THE GREAT MOTHER ASPECT."
A Treatise on Cosmic Fire, p66

"THE HUMAN AND THE DEVA EVOLUTIONS WILL MERGE. MAN EVOLVES BY CONTACT AND EXPERIENCE - EXPANDING. DEVAS EVOLVE BY LESSENING CONTACT - LIMITATION IS THE LAW FOR THEM. MAN AIMS AT SELF-CONTROL; DEVAS MUST ALLOW THEMSELVES TO BE CONTROLLED."
A Treatise on Cosmic Fire, p667

"MAN IS INNATELY LOVE PRODUCING COHERENCY; DEVAS ARE INNATELY INTELLIGENCE, PRODUCING ACTIVITY. MAN'S WILL SHOWS AS SELF-CONSCIOUSNESS; DEVAS WILL SHOWS AS CONSTRUCTIVE VIBRATION."
A Treatise on Cosmic Fire, p667

"THE HUMAN EVOLUTION SHOULD GIVE STRENGTH TO THE DEVA, AND THE DEVA JOY TO THE HUMAN. MAN SHOULD COMMUNICATE TO THE DEVAS THE OBJECTIVE POINT OF VIEW, WHILE THEY IN TURN WILL POUR IN TO HIM THEIR HEALING MAGNETISM. THEY ARE THE CUSTODIANS OF PRANA, MAGNETISM AND VITALITY, JUST AS MAN IS THE CUSTODIAN OF THE FIFTH PRINCIPLE, OR MANAS." (MANAS IS A SANSKRIT WORD MEANING 'MIND'.)
Letters on Occult Meditation, p183.

To return to the question of what I think makes the Findhorn essences unique, I would say there are key important elements in the making of a mother tincture. As well as attunement as described above (the consciousness of the person making the essence affects an essence-in-making) all elements need to be in balance and harmony; from the environment in which the plant or tree is growing (pristine is ideal), to the landscape and its energies, the cosmic and extra-planetary forces (for example new and full moons), etc.

So a remedy such as Gorse, made in this particular landscape, with pure Scottish water, and flowers that grow wild in an area of Findhorn known as "the Magic Triangle" and that can be in sunlight for more than eighteen hours a day, all this considered, it is understandable that Findhorn's Gorse flower essence contains a lot of light and therefore energy.

Making flower essences has led me on a journey of discovery into nature that opens my eyes and heightens my senses. I marvel at the beauty of nature all around me...

Healing with Flowers

SELECTING FLOWER ESSENCES

Successful flower essence selection begins, for me, in being able to identify key emotional, psychological and soul issues. This means bringing your awareness to an understanding of the presenting problems, as well as difficult or traumatic events in the past that continue to impact negatively on one or more of the bodies. Just as a person who is in shock may not be conscious of the fact they are in shock, so may we be unconscious – in a state of shock – in the wake of an adrenaline-triggered, acute reaction to a stressor.

In my practice I attune to and consider the following in a client: their overall physical health, energy levels, mental focus and clarity, predominant emotions and thought patterns, fears, self-esteem, motivation, life changes, relationships as well as relationship to work, sexuality, stress, sleep, shock or trauma and environmental influences, if any.

CHOOSING FOR YOURSELF

To select the essences, which would be most beneficial for you at this time, see which ones most closely address the positive qualities you would like to encourage. Look for key emotional, psychological and soul issues. Often your intuition will call your attention to particular flower essences. Read the descriptions and see which essences intuitively feel right. Other popular methods include dowsing with a pendulum, muscle testing and attuning using flower attunement cards.

TAKING FLOWER ESSENCES

Flower essences have a wide range of applications. Take several drops directly under the tongue or in a glass of water and sip throughout the day. Add them to bath water, creams or lotions, apply topically or spray them on your person, around the home and workplace. The essences are most effective when used frequently in small amounts. In times of crisis or transition, use them up to several times an hour. Individual essences may be blended together.

INSTRUCTIONS IN PREPARING A DOSE BOTTLE

Fill a clean dropper bottle with three parts pure water (e.g. purified or spring) to one part organic brandy alcohol and then add three or four drops each of the stock flower essences you have chosen. Shake well to disperse the essences into the water. These formulas will only keep for a few years. However, their shelf life can be extended by increasing the proportion of brandy to water (e.g. 1 part brandy and 2 parts water) or by keeping them in a refrigerator.

ABOUT DILUTIONS

You can take seven drops directly under the tongue, generally three times a day from ready-to-take 'dose' bottles. However, the drops can be administered more frequently in acute conditions and then reduced with improvement. For example, reduce to twice a day, morning and night, or once a day only if you desire to take the essence/s over a long period of time.

'Stock' dilution refers to the concentrated flower essence and it is generally the choice of therapists to prepare dose bottles, often by combining different single essences to create formulas or mixtures. However, single flower essences can also be used at this dilution. For babies and young children, and small animals, the number of drops can be reduced to half the adult dose essences or diluted in a little water.

Alternatively, apply a few drops to the pulse points on the wrist, behind the knees and the soles of the feet.

BE CREATIVE

Essences can also be added to bath water, creams and gels (such as aloe vera) and applied to the skin, or added to a mist spray and sprayed on the body or in the environment.

Original Tincture

Floral infusion

Mother Tincture

50% brandy alcohol to which is added 50% original tincture (floral infusion)

Stock Bottle

1/3 brandy alcohol + 2/3 pure water + 7 drops Mother Tincture

Dose Bottle

1/4 brandy alcohol + 3/4 pure water + 7 drops stock essence (ready to take)

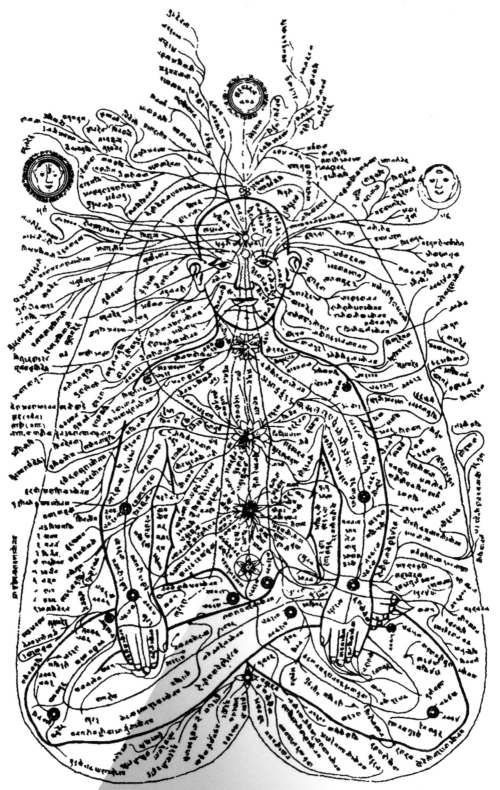

Tansley DV (1977)

The Chakras and Energy Medicine

THE SOUL IS THE HEALER WITHIN THE FORM AND TRUE SPIRITUAL HEALING COMES ABOUT THROUGH THE EVOCATION AND DOWN POURING OF THE SOUL'S ENERGY INTO THE ETHERIC VEHICLE SWEEPING IT INTO A NEW CONDITION OF BRILLIANCE, THUS CONDITIONING DIRECTLY THE DENSE PHYSICAL FORM.

ALICE BAILEY

Flower essences are vibrational remedies that influence the energetic patterns of body and soul and could be described as 'liquid drops of consciousness'. To understand how flower essences work, we need to recognise the multi-dimensional model of the human constitution of body, mind, soul and spirit.

'Vital forces', energy and electricity play a major role in the maintenance of physical life. In plants, for example, light is converted into chemical energy through the processes of photosynthesis. This energy is then used by the plant for all kinds of activities and functions. In the human being, vital life force or *prana* is taken in by and transmitted into the physical body by the etheric body.

The etheric body underlies and permeates the physical body and contains the energetic blueprint of our physical structure. It is the scaffolding upon which the physical body is constructed. The etheric body energises and stimulates the dense physical cells into activity. Also referred to as the vital body, it transmits energy to the physical body via a network of channels called *nadi*. *Nadi* (the Sanskrit for 'tube' or 'flow') are the channels through which, in traditional Indian medicine and spiritual science, the energies of the subtle body are said to flow. *Nadi* seem to correspond to the meridians of traditional Chinese medicine and are etheric counterparts of the nervous system. They connect at special points of intensity called *chakras*.

The word 'chakra' literally means 'wheel' implying that these force centres are wheels of energy. There are seven major chakras within the etheric body. These vibrate in high frequencies, each one at its own specific rate. Chakras evolve over time, from semi-dormancy to vibrant activity when fully developed. In advanced development, a chakra will perform higher functions. The chakras are responsible for the correct functioning of the entire human organism, producing both physiological and psychological effects. Chakras could be defined as biophysical resonators that activate the endocrine glands and maintain the health of the organ systems. The chakras take in, assimilate and process energy of higher vibrations. These energies are then blended and transformed to create the secondary energies needed to vitalise the body. The four major agents of distribution of the life energies are the etheric body, the endocrine system, the nervous system and the bloodstream, four aspects of one vital circulatory system which work as one integrated whole. Free circulation of the life essence is paramount to good health and wellbeing.

CHAKRA IMBALANCES

Chakras are subject to over-stimulation, under-stimulation and blockage. When chakras are blocked and the flow of life force is impeded, this can manifest as disturbances in physical, emotional or mental wellbeing. Our established dispositions and modes of being are reflected in the etheric body, which in turn have an impact on the physical organs via the endocrine glands and the chakras. For example, negative emotions such as anxiety, anger or jealousy suppress the activity of chakras. Our thoughts and emotions thereby arouse the glands and they mould, not only our temperament but our physical manifestation as well. As the chakras govern areas of the body and glands, healing energies may be effectively channelled through them and balance achieved with the aid of flower and vibrational essences.

THE SEVEN MAJOR CHAKRAS

The following summary of the major chakras (sometimes also referred to as "centres") gives their location and function.

THE BASE CHAKRA

The first chakra rules the physical will-to-be and self-preservation instincts. It supports all the other chakras, feeding the life-giving principle, the will-to-live, to all parts of the body, gives stability and security and provides conditions for basic human potentiality and fulfilment.

The energy of the base chakra is influenced by the earth element, densest of all the elements, being the mixture of the four other elements: water, fire, air, and ether. The earth element is connected with the desire for security in the form of shelter and livelihood. Located at the coccyx at the base of the spine, it governs elimination on all levels and externalises as the physical body's adrenal glands. The hormone adrenaline affects the body's water and salt balance, is responsible for regulating the flight or fight stress response, that helps us to sense danger and cope with stress, and governs the functioning of the kidneys and elimination, the spinal column, the skeletal system as a whole, the urinary system and lower intestine.

The base chakra is the harbour of our unconscious fears and instincts for survival as well as for success and achievement. A person who is dominated by the base chakra is obsessed by the desire to find security.

THE SACRAL CHAKRA

The second chakra concerns the pro-creation of life and self-perpetuation. It also governs personal education, family responsibility, comfort, food, sex and the creative use of money. Sacral energy has a magnetic quality and gives a person vitality and attractiveness. This centre is the seat of the element water and the astral plane. Water is the life-giving essence of life and is intimately connected with the moon, indicated by the influence of the lunar cycle on ocean tides and on our body chemistry and emotions. Sacral energies govern all the fluids of the body. Located at the base of the lumbar spine and level with the navel, the sacral *chakra* vitalises the sexual life, controlling the whole of the reproductive system and externalises in the physical body as the ovaries in the female and testes in the male. This centre governs the legs, specifically the hips and feet. The sacral *chakra* rules our desires for the highest enjoyment for excitement – in physical beauty, rhythmic movement and creativity. Once the sacral *chakra's* energies are transformed and expressed through its higher correspondence, the throat *chakra,* the creative process is translated into sound thoughts and pure speech, for example, through art, music and writing.

THE SOLAR PLEXUS CHAKRA

The third *chakra* is primarily a major receiving and 'composting' centre of emotional reactions, desire impulses and energies. It gathers in all the lower energies and is a focal point for direction and distribution, transferring them to the higher centres. Solar plexus energy governs the emotional body and rules primal instincts and desires. Fire in this *chakra* provides both light and heat, aiding in the digestion and absorption of food and supplying the whole body with the vital energy needed for survival. Fire is purifying and nourishing, but destructive when it gets out of control.

Located just below the level of the shoulder blades on the spine, the solar plexus *chakra* rules the regions of the gastrointestinal system – pancreas, stomach, liver, gall bladder and spleen. This *chakra* can be over-stimulated by emotional over-reactions and blocked when we are fearful of our own or other people's emotions. Ego pride in achievement occupies a large part of the consciousness of the person dominated by third *chakra* energy, who is motivated by the desire for recognition and power.

THE HEART CHAKRA

The fourth *chakra* anchors the life stream from the spiritual source and focuses the feeling consciousness of the soul, transforming energies from the personal to the transpersonal level. When developed, awareness shifts from individual consciousness (solar plexus *chakra*) to group consciousness and unconditional love and is then motivated by love, compassion and the desire for sharing. Through this centre we learn to radiate the energies of love flowing from the soul, out into the world.

The energy of the heart *chakra* is influenced by the element of air, circulating fresh oxygen and vital life force energy (*prana*).

Located in the region of the heart, its glandular counterpart is the thymus. It governs the heart, blood and circulatory system. It is also closely connected to the lungs and respiration, the spleen, and governs the immune system and the lymphatic glands of the body. Impeded circulation of this centre's vital energy of love leads to problems such as depression and cardiovascular imbalances. A person centred in heart *chakra* consciousness has overcome the preoccupations of the lower *chakras* – security (base), sensuality and sexuality (sacral), recognition and power (solar plexus).

THE THROAT CHAKRA

The fifth *chakra* focuses the creative consciousness of the soul. It promotes self-awareness through aspiration to help and serve our fellow human beings. The throat centre controls the adaptability of thoughts and ideas and when developed expresses through creative thought, speech and writing. This *chakra* is influenced by the element ether. The elements of earth, water, fire and air cease to have control over the person polarised in the consciousness of the throat *chakra*.

Its focal point of activity is the thyroid gland, which produces hormones that help to regulate the body's metabolism, the production of energy from the breakdown of food. The throat *chakra* governs the entire alimentary canal, the lungs and respiratory tract, the ears and the vocal apparatus.

Throat centre malfunctions occur when higher creativity is not properly expressed, doubt when knowledge is used unwisely, or by negative or rigid thinking. High stress can cause over-activity of the thyroid leading to 'burn out'. Criticism, whether voiced or not, severely affects this *chakra*.

THE AJNA CHAKRA

The sixth *chakra* gathers up energies from, and co-ordinates, all the *chakras* and is also responsible for determining our harmonious development. It is the distributing agent of the energy of active intelligence. The *ajna* or brow *chakra* embodies the idea lying behind the act of creation, directing the expression of the personality as it realises and distributes the spiritual energy of the soul. When developed, this centre focuses spiritual purpose, wisdom, insight and imagination, that are then directed through the personality.

The gland corresponding to the *ajna* is the pituitary. The double multiple petals of the lotus symbolising this *chakra* represent the anterior and posterior lobes of the pituitary gland. It governs primarily the lower brain and nervous system, ears, nose and the left eye, which is the eye of the personality or the lower self.

The element ether is associated with this *chakra,* being the combination of all the elements in their purest form. The solar and lunar nerve energies (*pingala* and *ida nadi*) intertwine up through all *chakras* and join into one at the *ajna chakra*.

THE CROWN CHAKRA

The seventh *chakra* is a centre of synthesis that links to the higher self, relating spirit and personality, and directs all the other *chakras.* As the seat of the soul, it is said to represent the spiritual will-to-be, and focuses the aspiration for spiritual purpose and a meaningful life. Located just above the top of the head,

this *chakra* governs the upper brain and right eye. It rules the pineal gland, which is electromagnetic and photosensitive. Although very little is known about the pineal's function, the hormone melatonin, secreted by the pineal gland, helps regulate other hormones and maintains the body's circadian rhythms.

THREE IMPORTANT MINOR CHAKRAS

The alta major *chakra,* spleen and vagus nerve centres are not major *chakras* but their function is as significant as are the major seven, and they are therefore listed here.

THE ALTA MAJOR CHAKRA

The alta major is a minor *chakra* but functions as a major. When fully developed, it forms a communication centre between vital *kundalini* energy of the spinal column and the energy of the crown and brow *chakras,* and leads to an acquired and conscious control of our *dharma* or soul's work on earth. It has the power to bring down intuitive vision into consciousness.

This centre has a major influence over the memories held in the cerebral cortex and is related to sleep and to the working out of past experiences in sleep.

Located at the back of the head at the base of the skull, the alta major, through its associated gland, has a commanding link with the most basic brain structure that is dedicated to physical survival – the brain stem and the cerebellum, which governs motor behaviour, controls autonomic, involuntary functions such as breathing, heart rate and blood pressure. It activates fight and flight reactions if danger is detected and also has a role in emotional calming.

THE SPLEEN

The spleen *chakra* is not a major *chakra.* However, it plays an important role in receiving and assimilating life force or *prana,* which is then distributed to the other *chakras* and through the endocrine glands and autonomic nervous system to the organs of the body.

Located at the back of the etheric body, close to and connected to the physical spleen, it governs the working of the body in the amount of life force available.

THE VAGUS NERVE

Although a minor *chakra,* it is of prime importance with regard to its purpose and action for those on the spiritual path. It is the pathway for the inner breath and the major pathway for information flowing down through the head *chakras.* This centre is the main centre, like the spleen *chakra,* for the reception of *prana.*

The vagus centre, which is controlled by the heart *chakra,* is located between the shoulder blades, just above the heart centre and the thymus. The vagus nerve is the largest nerve in the parasympathetic nervous system (which activates involuntary muscles that restore the body's energy); it commences in the medulla oblongata and midbrain and extends downwards to embrace the heart, lungs and other parts of the thorax.

The heart centre, once active, stimulates the head *chakras* through the vagus nerve. When this centre is rhythmic and flowing, the nervous system will work efficiently and effectively. When over or under-stimulated this will lead to physical nervous problems.

FLOW OF ENERGIES FROM THE SUBTLE BODIES TO THE PHYSICAL BODY

Two streams of energy convey the life force, or *pranas,* through the etheric body into the physical body. The *pranas* pertaining to intelligence, the consciousness stream, flow into the *nadis,* the fine etheric channels that underlie the nerves. The *pranas* pertaining to the sustenance of the form nature, the life aspect, flow into the endocrine system from the seven major *chakras* via their externalised endocrine glands, and through the hormones into the bloodstream.

HOW FLOWER ESSENCES WORK

Flower essences are absorbed through the mucus membranes in the mouth and enter directly into the bloodstream. The vibrational imprint of the essences is then transmitted through the bloodstream, influencing the endocrine system, the nervous system, the *nadis* and the *chakras.*

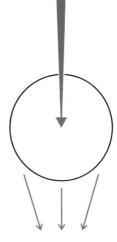

INCOMING
PRIMARY ENERGY

NADIS

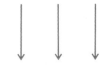

NERVOUS SYSTEM

ENDOCRINE SYSTEM

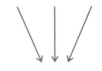

BLOOD

Flower Essences

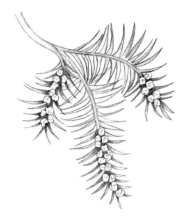

REALISE YOUR LIFE'S PURPOSE.
CAST OFF BURDENS THAT HOLD
YOU BACK AND TAKE SPONTANEOUS
ACTION THAT LEADS TO NEW
DIRECTIONS FOR GROWTH.

ANCIENT YEW
Taxus

EMERGENCE

The yew is the longest-lived tree in the world, dating back two hundred million years. It is a symbol of everlasting life and perpetual renewal and transformation. Ancient yew flower essence can assist in letting go of whatever is standing in the way of achieving your soul purpose.

The soul is a vehicle and a catalyst for the energies of life and consciousness and is the life force of evolution itself. The soul is light and this inner light can illuminate your life so that you see clearly. From expanded awareness, you remember who you are and where you are going in life. In that light you can see where you are going, and what must be done.

When you come to the realisation that the time has come to release your attachment to someone or something that is holding you back, like the irrepressible yew tree you are propelled onwards to change, adapt, and make choices and that will allow you to be free to grow, expand and regenerate.

As new possibilities emerge, you can intuitively choose the path that leads in the right direction and which is in harmony with your soul's plan.

ATTRIBUTES

▸ Follow your heart and trust
▸ Realise your soul potential and destiny
▸ Stimulate mental perceptiveness and agility
▸ Assisting the memory and powers of recall
▸ Cutting the ties that bind you to the past
▸ Allow probabilities to emerge naturally

INDICATIONS

▸ Losing sight of your life's true direction and purpose
▸ Fixed patterns of thought and behaviour
▸ Dependent attachments to something or someone
▸ Obstacles to personal growth and development
▸ Outmoded patterns of being that hold you back
▸ Burdens that weigh down your progression

AFFIRMATION: I know who I am and where I am going. I emerge triumphant.

CROSS REFERENCE

Blocks | Breakthrough | Change | Freedom | Goal | Habit patterns | Karma | Memory
Non-attachment | Purpose | Relationship | Release | Surrender | Thinking/Thought
patterns | Transformation | Will

FOCUS ON YOUR PURPOSE WITH
ENTHUSIASM AND PERSEVERANCE,
AND USE YOUR WILL TO REALISE
THE GOAL.

APPLE
Malus

PURPOSE

In the language of flowers, apple blossom has the meaning of 'temptation', which
may hark back to the biblical myth of the 'forbidden fruit'. Temptation is a charac-
teristic featured in the essence of apple. This flower essence is an aid to realising
your objectives by focusing the mind and mobilising the will through your intention.
Apple essence is an aid to realising your goals and objectives by cultivating an open
attitude and willing body and mind. With willingness, and the power of sustained
application, you can pursue a goal without getting sidetracked or procrastinating.
Procrastination is a form of self-sabotage that can lead to frustration and disap-
pointment and creates inner resistance that hinders good self-management.
Apple essence can help you to realise your objectives when you clarify and focus
on your purpose and intention. You can joyfully and willingly command your inner
forces and impulses towards the power of sustained application to live up to your
highest goal.

- Clarity of purpose and intention
- Determination and perseverance to stick to your resolutions
- Mastery and direction of willpower
- Power to direct your energies into productive action
- Passion and diligence
- Internalising your intentions and acting on them

INDICATIONS

- Driving impulses that lead you to distraction
- Lack of direction and purposeful intention
- Difficulty in sustaining one-pointed focus
- Need of self-management and willpower
- Procrastination sabotages your objective
- Dissipating your energies

AFFIRMATION I align myself with my higher purpose and act for the good of all.

CROSS REFERENCE

Action I Addiction I Avoidance I Commitment I Discipline I Enthusiasm I Focus I Goal
Lethargy I Motivation I Passion I Perseverance I Power I Procrastination I Purpose
Resistance I Responsibility I Self-sabotage I Will

NURTURE YOURSELF AND
OTHERS THROUGH LOVE AND
INTIMACY. OVERCOME FEELINGS
OF SEPARATENESS. EMANATE
AND ATTRACT WARMTH AND
TENDERNESS

BALSAM
Impatiens glandulifera

TENDERNESS

Balsam is a medicinal plant native to India and prized by Victorian gardeners.
Balsam's English name 'touch-me-not' could refer to its seed vessel, which scatters
its seeds to a distance by a spontaneous movement. In the language of flowers its
meaning is, "I am sensitive, don't touch".

Balsam flower personifies the nurturing, feminine aspect of the self, and love and
acceptance of your being in physical form. Love yourself, and your love will radiate
out and touch others.

The balsam personality 'type' is a self-sacrificing server and can become distanced
from deeply connecting with others on the physical level. They can be out of touch
with their own feelings and needs, and often put the needs of others before their
own. Distancing oneself from physical or intimate personal contact with others
can cut us off from truly feeling. Such barriers are dissolved when we can express
loving contact with others.

Touch allows us to share deep feelings in ways that can be more powerful than
words. On the highest level, touch governs healing, as our hands are powerful
energy centres that channel healing from the plane of spiritual love. Feelings of
warmth and tenderness guide the soul in touch with the true self, bringing forth
the sacredness of our being in physical form.

- Easy expression of love and intimacy
- Natural affection and tenderness without reservation
- Emotional availability
- Unconditional patience and understanding
- Relationship bonding
- Being in touch with your creative feminine power

INDICATIONS

- Repressed sensitivity to feeling/touch
- Reduced physical warmth and presence
- Distanced from feeling contact with others
- Emotional walls and barriers that curtail love's expression
- Over-detachment from the feeling sense creates inhibitions
- Alienation from the mother or nurturing, feminine aspect of self

AFFIRMATION: I am happy and at home in my body and the world.

CROSS REFERENCE

Abandonment | Alienation | Aloofness | Birth and Birthing | Blocks | Body | Bonding
Feminine principle | Fertility | Intimacy | Love | Nurturing | Openness | Out-of-body
Passion | Patience | Rejection | Relationship | Repression | Self-harm | Self-love | Sensitivity
Sensuality | Separation | Sexuality | Tenderness

BELL HEATHER
Erica cinerea

CONFIDENCE

Bell heather grows happily in harsh habitats including heathland and acidic soils. While delicate in appearance, it is hardy and symbolises consistency and persistence. By standing firmly grounded and focusing on the positive aspects of a situation, you can mobilise your inner forces to persevere, and find the confidence to keep moving forward.

The stress of being dislodged from your secure standpoint, and the anxiety of not knowing what is coming, can lead to fear of losing control over the outcome of a situation. As a consequence, common sense may be suppressed, judgement impaired and you are left feeling exposed, defenceless and helpless. Bell Heather essence may help to let go of anxiety, turmoil and fear of the unknown. You can admit and endure change, knowing that everything in life and in nature is constantly changing and growing.

When you realise and calmly embrace the knowing that everything in life is in constant change, you will be able to overcome any adversity through faith and trust in yourself. By focusing on the positive aspects of a situation, you adapt and come to terms with change, and thereby manage difficult situations more effectively. When you confidently remain in the not-knowing present moment, you are released from the pressure of needing everything to be all right, right now.

ATTRIBUTES

- Belief in yourself and your ability to deal with any situation
- Consolidate your energies and stand your ground
- Manage stress effectively and confidently
- Move forward with trust and conviction
- Grounded and centred
- Inner strength and resilience

INDICATIONS

- The anxiety of feeling insecure and uncertain
- Fear of losing control of a situation
- Fragile, unsettled and 'off your centre'
- Impaired judgement and discernment
- Doubt and uncertainty
- Numbed and dazed after a shake up

AFFIRMATION: I stand firmly and securely in my being.
I have faith and trust in myself.

CROSS REFERENCE

Anxiety I Calm I Centering I Change I Confidence I Control I Crisis I Emergency I Faith
Flexibility I Grounding I Perseverance I Shock I Strength I Stress I Trauma I Trust

BIRCH
Betula pendula

VISION

In the Celtic tradition, birch is one of the seven sacred trees and one of the three pillars of wisdom, along with oak and yew. Birch's wisdom teaches us to be open-minded, thereby allowing our thoughts and ideas to flow more easily.

We perceive the world though our individual 'lenses', through thoughts, impressions, ideas, emotions and sensations. But an egocentric bias can occur when we think of the world from our own point of view too much, and assume it to be a definitive evidence of reality.

When fixed ideas are present, clear perception is limited. Birch flower essence allows us to look at events with fresh eyes and from different perspectives by helping us to open our minds and free our imagination. It also helps us to expand our capacity to visualise and find creative routes to desired goals by releasing our expectations of how we think things should be. Birch shows us that, while knowledge helps us to see and understand things as they are, it is the imagination that allows us to see things as they could be.

With birch, we learn to transcend mental limitations and continue to grow and learn. By expanding our perceptions, we garner positive aspirations that broaden our awareness and encourage novel, varied and exploratory thoughts and actions.

New thinking habits that broaden the mind and our imaginative capacity

Open-minded exploration of creative routes to desired goals

Focused attitude and intention in problem solving

Shifting of perspectives in order to overcome obstacles

Power to see the vision and direct one's course to it

Develop the faculty of creative visualisation

INDICATIONS

Self-limiting, predetermined thought patterns and problem-solving strategies

Lack of imagination

Narrow-minded thinking, fixed ideas and 'blind spots'

Stuck in thought patterns that inhibit creative thinking

Worry clouding the way forward

Preconceived expectations foster misconceptions and false conclusions

AFFIRMATION: I open my mind to new ways and understanding.

CROSS REFERENCE

Awareness | Clarity | Confusion | Delusion | Discernment | Focus | Illusion | Inspiration
Perception | Receptivity | Thinking/Thought | Patterns | Understanding | Unconscious
mind | Universal mind | Vision | Worry

CLEAR YOUR MIND AND FOCUS YOUR THINKING. DISPEL EMOTIONAL TURMOIL THAT HINDERS YOUR POWERS OF CONCENTRATION.

BROOM
Cytisus scoparius

CLARITY

Broom was at one time a common herbal treatment for many ailments and disorders. The origin of the name refers to a sweeping branch, and is regarded by
shamans to be a superior ritual broom in space clearing for sweeping away any
unwanted energies.

Broom flower essence may help to clear and bring light into the mind, supporting
the mental body's capacity in learning, concentration, memory and recall. This new
brightness frees up the thinking process thereby supporting creative thinking.
Emotional agitation and anxiety makes it difficult to think clearly and quickly.
This in turn affects the mental processes of comprehension, learning, planning and
decision-making. Clear thinking gives us the confidence and power to correctly
comprehend impressions and ideas. The ability to create and communicate ideas is
a defining quality of the human mind.

Broom essence helps to illuminate the mind so that the enhanced power of intuitive perception and abstract thinking become more flexible and adaptable.
As patterns of abstract light are rendered down into ideas, we are able to apply
and express our thoughts through creative, intelligent activity.

- Confident mental performance and memory recall
- Building powers of concentration and mental endurance
- Think clearly and make decisions quickly
- Understand the essence of perceived ideas
- Power to focus and apply mental imagery
- Assisting the creative construction of thought forms

INDICATIONS

- Difficulty communicating thoughts clearly and directly
- Mental confusion or agitation
- Impediment to focusing the mind on one thing at a time
- Poor concentration
- Mental fatigue or overwhelm
- Not integrating or applying your intellectual understanding

AFFIRMATION: My mind is clear. I express myself,
my thoughts, and ideas with ease.

CROSS REFERENCE

Attention I Attunement I Clarity I Communication I Comprehension I Concentration
Confusion I Decision I Focus I Forgetfulness I Inspiration I Intuition I Knowledge I Learning
Light I Memory I Thinking/Thought patterns I Writing

CABBAGE
Brassica oleracea

DEVOTION

Cabbage has been cultivated for more than four thousand years. Hippocrates, the 'father of medicine', Pythagoras and other learned philosophers have paid tribute to the great virtues of cabbage. It is also worth mentioning that the humble cabbage brought fame to the Findhorn Foundation community.

There's a well-known saying, "without vision, the people perish". A vision calls for action, reveals a plan, and ends in a purpose. It inspires enthusiasm, creating focus and a sense of direction. Motivation and enthusiasm can peter out when there is a lack of vision or purpose and it can be hard going to sustain your effort, let alone muster the enthusiasm for other tasks and projects.

Cabbage flower essence motivates and encourages you to follow your vision. By trusting 'the flow' of events, the vision can manifest perfectly and in right timing. Vision is the singular most differentiating attribute of effective leaders. True leaders in any area 'hold the vision' of what life could be like for the good of everyone involved. Cabbage fosters work as 'love in action' and by your actions and commitment, inspires you and others onwards. Cabbage's dynamism may assist to harness enthusiasm, patience, persistence and perseverance.

ATTRIBUTES

- Positively and dynamically focus your energies
- Strong motivation and commitment to your vision
- Feeling connected rather than an individual body
- Enthusiasm helps hard work become easier
- Power to take command and direct an enterprise
- Strengthening individuality with group cohesiveness and co-operation

INDICATIONS

- Lack of vision and purpose hinders your ability to apply yourself
- Aimless labouring leads to feeling ineffective
- Joyless labouring: "It's too difficult!"
- Holding an attitude of 'I can do it alone, myself'
- Weary from pushing yourself too hard and not pacing yourself
- The tension of 'holding the vision' becomes a weight and a burden

AFFIRMATION: I am focused and clear. I accomplish my mission with ease and joy.

CROSS REFERENCE

Action | Commitment | Concentration | Discipline | Enthusiasm | Fatigue | Focus | Goal
Leadership | Lethargy | Manifestation | Motivation | Perseverance | Procrastination
Purpose | Relationship | Spiritual connection | Strength | Vision | Vitality | Will | Workaholic

BE OPEN-HEARTED AND OPEN-
MINDED. TRANSCEND NEGATIVE,
INHERITED PREDISPOSITIONS
AND CONSCIOUSLY CONDUCT
YOURSELF WITH INTEGRITY AND
IN THE SPIRIT OF GOODWILL.

CHERRY
Prunus serrulata

COMPASSION

Cherry blossom symbolises the philosophy of balance, harmony and co-existence, where seemingly separate or opposing forces are interconnected and interdepend-ent in the natural world. These complementary opposites interact constantly and are able to transform each other to promote stabilisation similar to homeostasis.

Cherry is an essence that addresses strong polarities. The duality between the inner forces within the psyche of spirit (self/consciousness) and phenomena (mat-ter/nature) are bound together as parts of a mutual whole and are in continual change and mutual adjustment. When you oppose one side of your existence, tensions or resistance inherent in the relationship create inner conflict and you become unbalanced.

Many of us have unconscious patterns of becoming polarised, due to past and learned experiences and inherited tendencies. Stress and conflict can push us over the edge into over-identifying with one side of the pole at the expense of the other. This essence may help to neutralise and harmonise the two inner opposing sides. Achieving a state of wholeness or 'at-one-ment' involves acceptance of all that we are, without judgement. As we radiate loving kindness with an open and compas-sionate heart, we expand our ability to love and be loved. As a consequence, we realise that every moment of life is precious, that we need to live life to the full and cherish every moment.

- Heart and mind working in harmony and unity
- Let the heart guide you in your relationships
- Intuitive empathy with your own and others' feelings
- Unconditional love that overcomes any difficulty or conflict
- Relax, be cheerful and enjoy the present
- Loving kindness guided by heartfelt understanding

INDICATIONS

- Polarised into two competing dualistic positions
- Inflexible, uncompromising view or attitude
- Reduced sensitivity to feelings
- Negative and argumentative patterns of relating to others
- Judging yourself and others
- Imbalance puts you on the offensive

AFFIRMATION: My heart is open to love and compassion for myself, and others.

CROSS REFERENCE

Acceptance I Bonding I Compassion I Flexibility I Habit patterns I Heartache I Hostility
Intolerance I Judgemental I Karma I Male/female balance I Negativity I Obstinate I Polarity
Reconciliation I Relationship I Resentment I Rigidity I Sensitivity I Tension I Unconditional
love I Understanding

STAY CALM AND FOCUSED. OVERCOME
AGITATION AND ANXIETY AND FIND
YOUR CENTRE OF BALANCE.

DAISY
Bellis perennis

PROTECTION

The medicinal properties of daisy have been recorded as far back as the 16th century. A popular remedy with a wide range of applications, it has also been used in treating delicate and listless children. Daisy has traditionally been associated with children and is a symbol for innocence, purity and enduring love. It also represents survival due to its ability to persist and endure, even when trampled on.

A crisis will impact the physical, emotional and mental bodies and in cases of extreme shock or trauma, there may be dissociation between body and mind, the so-called 'out of body' experience. In esoteric psychology this is called a 'cleavage' and can occur between any of the bodies.

Daisy flower essence may help you to stay centred, grounded and in command when circumstances which are out of your control threaten to throw you off balance. This essence helps you to centre in yourself, remain calm and composed, collect your thoughts, notice the body's defence reactions.

Awareness and objectivity enables you to then move forward with calm, firmly rooted in the earthly realms. Nothing can faze you when you are centred and grounded in the self, from which the sense of safety, balance and order arise naturally.

- Centred and grounded
- Sure-footed, stable passage through difficult times
- Emotional safety and security
- Composed and unperturbed no matter what
- Stay on purpose and on course
- Childlike trust and openness

INDICATIONS

- Inner turmoil throwing you off balance
- Feeling overwhelmed leads to confusion
- Losing command of your sensibilities when stressed
- Emotional tension and agitation
- 'Out of body' experience related to trauma or shock
- Faltering and insecure

AFFIRMATION: I am calm and centred and feel safe in my world.

CROSS REFERENCE

Adolescence I Anxiety I Calm I Centering I Concentration I Confusion I Grounding
Hysteria I Inner child I Insecurity I Mood swing I Nervousness I Openness I Out-of-body
Overwhelm I Playfulness I Protection I Sexual abuse I Shock I Shyness I Stress I Trauma
Vulnerability

BE THE LIGHT AND BEAUTIFUL
BEING THAT YOU TRULY ARE. RELAX
THE DESIRE FOR PERFECTION AND
STIMULATE YOUR NATURAL POWERS
OF REGENERATION AND RENEWAL.
REVEAL YOUR YOUTHFULNESS
AND VITALITY.

ELDER
Sambucus nigra

BEAUTY

The first recorded medicinal use of elder dates back almost 2,500 years to Hippocrates, the father of medicine. Elder has been regarded as the medicine chest of country folk due to the large variety of herbal medications that are derived from the plant.

Elder expresses a serene, wise energy. The flower essence stimulates powers of recovery and renewal of the vital life energies that rejuvenate. When body and soul are revitalised, you can be imbued with the sense of wellbeing that boosts vitality and self-esteem.

Negative self-perceptions, poor self image and stuck emotions weigh down on body, mind and soul. The aging process can also lead to a poor self-image. If you do not feel good about yourself, the stress placed on your body as a result of your unhappiness will affect your overall wellbeing. How you appear is a direct reflection of how you see yourself, what you believe about your appearance, and how you feel about your body. Energy follows thought.

Elder essence opens the inner eye to the beauty that is within – for the experience of beauty is being in balance and harmony with your true nature. Thus empowered, your inner beauty radiates through you as youthful vitality and wellbeing.

ATTRIBUTES

Stimulate inner powers of recovery and recuperation

Open to a more vital precipitation of the life force

Connect with feelings of vitality and youthfulness

Reveal and radiate your inner beauty

Joyful expression of the physical body

Maintain a good self-image

INDICATIONS

Anxieties about yourself and your appearance

Feeling heavy, subdued or congested

Low personal vitality and dynamism

Poor self-image or self-esteem

Not comfortable in your body

Fear of ageing

AFFIRMATION: I am renewed and revitalised.
I radiate the beauty and joy of my wellbeing.

CROSS REFERENCE

Adolescence I Ageing I Body I Burnout I Confidence I Energy I Fatigue I Immunity I Inner child I Joy I Lethargy I Life force I Lightness I Nurturing I Perfectionism I Rejuvenation Self-acceptance I Self-criticism I Self-esteem I Self-harm I Self-image I Self-love Sensuality I Vitality

MAGNETISE YOUR ABILITIES TO RECEIVE AND TRANSMIT SPIRITUAL ENERGIES AND FORCES. BE A CLEAR CHANNEL THROUGH PURITY OF MOTIVE, RIGHT ALIGNMENT AND ATTUNEMENT.

ELECAMPANE
Inula helenium

SENSITIVITY

Elecampane radiates power and strength of purpose. It is a formidable transmitter-receiver of life force or *prana*. One of its common names is elfwort and growing it in your garden is supposed to attract fairies!

It may be helpful to souls who are developing intuitive powers and the higher psychic faculties. Elecampane flower essence is of benefit in connecting with the inner dimension of one's spirituality and channelling the higher energies in a balanced way.

Super-sensory perception of subtle etheric and spiritual energies for intuitive insight demands inner training and deep attunement. It is not unlike learning to play a musical instrument. First of all you have to tune your instrument.

There are potential dangers, however, in opening up to these higher energies. The sensitive soul can be highly impressionable to over-stimulation of the energy centres, becoming ungrounded and unstable, as well as susceptible to depletion and over-whelm. In the extreme, it can result in obsession.

Therefore, alignment to the soul, purity of motive and the discriminative loving power of the heart need to be engaged. The ability of knowing through direct perception gives intuitive insights that can be applied to spiritual work and practice. When the channels and receptors are clear, you are able to correctly register, integrate and transmit the higher vibrations. This is commitment to responsible and ethical chan-nelling of the energies of love and healing. These energies are then conducive to the progress of the person who rightly uses them to aid themselves and others. Elecam-pane flower essence gives confidence in the mastery of receiving, integrating and applying high spiritual vibrations.

- Strengthening and grounding inner spiritual connections
- Focus psychic faculties of impression, intuition and telepathy
- Ability to perceive finer energies and their vibrations
- Power to magnetise and transmit spiritual energies
- Exercise discrimination and care in the source of energies
- Calmness and confidence; connection and communication

INDICATIONS

- Overly-impressionable to low-level psychic phenomena
- Unstable and not grounded
- Indiscriminate use of psychic faculties and powers
- Exposure to astral forces through unstable emotional body
- Glamour or illusion from diffused connection to the spirit
- Limited awareness or connection leading to false interpretation

AFFIRMATION I channel Spiritual Love, Light and Power in service to the One.

CROSS REFERENCE

Alignment I Attunement I Awareness I Communication I Discrimination I Dream and Dreaming I Empowerment I Grounding I Higher self I Illusion I Intuition I Knowledge Perception I Power I Receptivity I Sensitivity I Spiritual connection I Vision I Wisdom

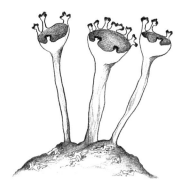

ELF CUP LICHEN
Cladonia coccifera

LIBERATION

Lichens are a combination of fungi and algae growing together in symbiosis. Most lichens live from the air. They are very sensitive to pollution, making them natural monitors of air quality, and are also resistant to radiation. The two organisms, fungi and algae, work as one and need each other to survive.

Symbiosis, a term adopted from biology, is a mutually beneficial relationship between two systems. It has been applied in Jungian psychology to describe the co-operative nature of the relationship between the personality or ego, and the self or soul. The premise is that emotional health can be maintained by having conscious awareness of, and strengthening, this relationship.

The unconscious mind is composed of hidden aspects of the self that continue to work on consciousness, influencing thought and behaviour although one is mostly not aware of them. These unconscious tendencies can be very powerful and even go against our conscious will.

Suppression of the unconscious shadow self will just increase its strength. Lying below the surface, it manifests in a sinister way by triggering memories on deeper levels of awareness. If continually repressed, it grows like a cancer, or inflames the problem, for example, when one suddenly gets very angry.

Elf Cup Lichen essence can help you to become clear of your past patterns of reaction. As a reminder that an issue will not just go away if you ignore it, it can help to release and purify negative emotional reactions and detrimental behaviour that cause pain and suffering. As the eminent psychologist Carl Gustav Jung pointed out, integration of the unconscious invariably has a healing effect.

ATTRIBUTES

- Dealing with old issues and patterns that can no longer be avoided
- Healthy release of deep-seated emotions
- Creating space for change and growth
- Allowing feelings with a deep sense of acceptance
- Owning disliked parts of yourself
- Becoming clear of your past patterns of reaction

INDICATIONS

- Deep-seated, imprinted emotional pain or trauma
- Suppressed emotions e.g. anger, sadness, shame or guilt
- Old issues that can no longer be avoided
- Reactive, out of control emotions
- Concealment or suppression of feelings by denial or disapproval
- Difficult to access negative patterns of reaction

AFFIRMATION: I cleanse and purify my emotional body of that which no longer serves the whole.

CROSS REFERENCE

Acceptance | Anger | Avoidance | Blocks | Catharsis | Cleansing | Denial | Frustration Guilt | Habit patterns | Integration | Irritability | Karma | Release | Repression | Resistance Sexual abuse | Shadow self | Shame | Unconscious mind

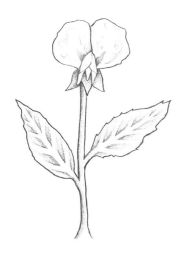

CULTIVATE CONFIDENT, ARTICULATE
SELF-EXPRESSION. RELEASE
NEGATIVE THOUGHT PATTERNS AND
CLEAR THE BLOCKS TO HEARTFELT
COMMUNICATION. SPEAK YOUR TRUTH.

GARDEN PEA
Pisum sativum

EXPRESSION

Pea is one of the oldest known vegetables and fossil remains have been found dating back to the Bronze Age. It symbolises respect and admiration in the language of flowers.

All creativity comes from within as inspiration, and is a gift. Garden pea flower essence helps you to construct a framework and strategy through which to express creatively. Self-confidence and belief in yourself is one of the first steps to success. People who are passionately engaged with their talent may become detached from the creative experience when negative thinking, self-doubt and criticism consumes the mind and the emotions. Garden pea flower essence helps in releasing negative self-talk that can lead to despair.

Expressing yourself creatively is an essential aspect of living a life of passion, fulfilment and authenticity. This essence can help you to construct a support system for self-expression and communication by opening pathways for your imagination to follow, and for beauty and inspiration to flow freely and spontaneously.

ATTRIBUTES

Strengthen the art and gift of creativity

Communicate your wisdom and talents with gentle power

Confident, hopeful and lighter attitude around creative projects

Develop a strong and positive self-belief

Having the courage to speak up for yourself

Embodying the beauty of your artistic expression

INDICATIONS

Obstacles to expressing yourself

Depression of the spirits associated with stifled creativity

Self-doubt and negative self-talk

Over-sensitive to criticism from others

Insecure and doubting your talent and ability

Attention seeking or approval seeking behaviour

AFFIRMATION I bring beauty in a new wave of conscious creativity.

CROSS REFERENCE

Acceptance | Blocks | Bullying | Communication | Confidence | Creativity | Criticism
Defensiveness | Empowerment | Expression | Frustration | Inferiority | Inner child
Insecurity | Motivation | Negativity | Rebelliousness | Repression | Self-esteem | Self-image
Self-sabotage | Sensitivity | Speaking | Victim | Writing

BE ENLIGHTENED AND ALLOW THE POWER OF THE LIFE FORCE TO RADIATE THROUGH YOU. RHYTHMIC FLOW OF LIFE FORCE HELPS HARMONISE MENTAL AND EMOTIONAL BODIES AND REGULATES YOUR RESPONSIVENESS TO LIGHT.

GINKGO
Ginkgo biloba

ENDURANCE

Ginkgo biloba is one of the oldest trees and geological records indicate this plant has grown on earth for 150 million years. It has been used in traditional medicine for thousands of years. Scientific studies have found evidence to support the medicinal use of ginkgo as an aid to increase circulation and enhance memory.

As a flower essence, it helps to regulate the body's responsiveness to light by magnetising the photosensitive mechanisms of the etheric pineal gland. The ancient Greeks understood the pineal gland's connection to the realms of thought, the connecting link between spiritual and physical worlds. Descartes claimed it to be the 'seat of the soul'.

Spiritual will, or the will to BE, manifesting as light, is conducted through the crown *chakra,* through the brain via the pineal gland, and into the heart *chakra.* It brings the strength and power of the life-giving force into the body.

Stress, worry and anxiety can disrupt the natural, rhythmic flow and coordination of the incoming streams of life-giving energy, leading to a loosening of the connection between body and mind. Contraction of the channels (*nadi*) through which the activity of these energies flow, leads to mental and emotional restlessness. It also affects the nervous and circulatory systems and disturbs mental equilibrium.

Ginkgo flower essence may be helpful in making the connections that allow the proper streaming of the life-giving energies. The power of the light force, penetrating into the mind, brings mental clarity, as equilibrium of the rhythm of life, and cycles, are maintained.

ATTRIBUTES

- Maintaining biorhythmic equilibrium
- Grounded awareness and thinking
- Evoking the light of the conscious mind
- Coherent, coordinated thinking and reasoning
- Clear powers of judgement, association, and recall
- Persistent endurance and connectivity

INDICATIONS

- Mental and emotional restlessness or dissociation
- Difficulty in concentrating or making decisions
- Contraction of the etheric channels (*nadi*)
- Mental confusion and emotional disengagement
- Disturbed sleep patterns and biorhythms
- Deviating, intermittent abstraction of the mind

AFFIRMATION: I align and connect. I stand in the Light of Truth.

CROSS REFERENCE

Aging I Anxiety I Apathy I Attention I Awareness I Blocks I Clarity I Communication Comprehension I Concentration I Confusion I Darkness I Decision I Discrimination I Dream and Dreaming I Forgetfulness I Grounding I Integration I Life force I Light I Memory Restlessness I Sleep patterns I Thinking /Thought patterns I Winter blues

CONNECT WITH YOUR POWERS OF
PATIENCE, PERSISTENCE AND
PERSEVERANCE. LETTING GO OF
UNNECESSARY BURDENS WILL SET
YOU FREE AND ULTIMATELY SERVES
THE HIGHEST GOOD.

GLOBETHISTLE
Echinops sphaerocephalus

STRENGTH

Globethistle has been used as a medicinal plant since ancient times. It is very attractive to bees, butterflies and all types of pollinating insects. In the language of flowers the thistle is an ancient symbol of nobility of character. Its 'signature' is that of commanding strength, resilience and integrity.

The globethistle personality 'type' is very magnetic, and is a champion of causes. Taking control of practical matters is an automatic impulse, as is the willingness to step forward and take charge.

Prolonged self-sacrificing service to others can result in your easily becoming overwhelmed, feeling 'put upon' or, in the extreme, the martyr. The demands of constantly taking responsibility for 'meeting the need' to the exclusion of acknowledging your own needs, may leave you feeling your life has become exhausting and unsatisfying. Attempts to correct the balance by trying to establish emotional boundaries can lead you to withdraw into yourself.

Globethistle flower essence can help to reconnect with your power, to distance yourself sufficiently to be able to see the whole picture and to see what needs to be done. It also helps in identifying patterns of behaviour that do not serve you or those you serve, and that can be sacrificed 'for the good of the whole'.

This essence teaches that when personal power and soul force are blended, the spirit of abundant, unconditional love and care-giving from the heart brings more life, energy and resources for you to actually do what needs to be done and feel a sense of joy and fulfilment.

- Knowing your limitations and honouring your own needs
- Giving unconditional service from the heart, joyfully and willingly
- Greater reserves of patience and flexibility
- As diligent in meeting your own needs as you are in meeting the needs of others
- Healthy yet flexible boundaries
- Willingness to go beyond self-interest and give of yourself for the good of the other

INDICATIONS

- In attempting to serve others, your life has become exhausting and unsatisfying
- Taking on the role of martyr or feeling you are being taken advantage of
- Over-developed sense of obligation and responsibility
- Over-giving leads to negative emotions of irritation, impatience and criticism
- Emotionally distancing yourself when overwhelmed
- Behaviours that keep people in a dependency relationship with you

AFFIRMATION: I am strong and whole. I serve joyfully in the spirit of goodwill.

CROSS REFERENCE

Addiction | Altruism | Co-dependence | Criticism | Flexibility | Freedom | Guilt | Habit patterns | Irritability | Non-attachment | Overwhelm | Patience | Perseverance | Resentment | Responsibility | Rigidity | Self-pity | Self-sabotage | Strength | Temper | Tolerance | Victim | Workaholic

GOLDEN IRIS
Iris pseudacorus

FIDELITY

Iris comes from the Greek word for rainbow, which is a symbol of the connection between spirit and matter. Anatomically, the iris controls the amount of light that enters the eye and it is a fact that the eye's iris reacts to emotions. Seeing something beautiful, for example, will make you open your eyes to let in more light.
Iris is also a symbol for the *ajna* or brow *chakra,* sometimes called the 'third eye', and is the seat of mind and intelligence. It coordinates the five spinal *chakras* and distributes the spiritual energy of the soul. This centre comes into full functioning activity when the personality and soul are in alignment. Golden Iris flower essence helps to connect with our divine light and reminds us that the key to inner peace can only be realised through alignment with the soul and spirit within.
When you are loyal to the purpose and principles of your true self, and sincere in your aspiration to live your life integrated with and guided by that, you can differentiate between what is real and what is unreal. Dedicated to moving forward regardless of the reactions of your lower nature, you are able to see the inner reality and the subjective meaning behind life and events. As you stand in the spiritual authority of the true self with this clear perception, you take right action recognising that 'energy follows thought'. You take command, thinking, seeing and conducting yourself as the soul.

Powers of discernment and seeing the truth

To live in the present and see your direction from a higher perspective

Integration and coordination of ego and psyche

Vigilance over inner drives and impulses

Ability to be the 'observer' and to see the reality of your dilemma

Opening the inner eye to inspiration and intuitive vision

Confused thinking and unruly emotions that inhibit right perception

A sense of duality, of being divided in different directions

Clear vision and discernment impaired by flawed thinking and/or emotional reactions

Obscured vision that creates limitations

Torn between the duality of individuality and unity

Lack of alignment leads to not acting from the authority and wisdom of your true self

AFFIRMATION: I stand in the light of truth. I am true to myself.

Alignment I Attunement I Awareness I Channelling I Concentration I Discrimination
Decision I Duality I Empowerment I Higher I Self I Inspiration I Integration I Intuition I Light
Non-attachment I Perception I Polarity I Self-realisation I Spiritual connection I Spiritual
emergence I Thinking/Thought pattern I Understanding I Universal mind I Vision I Wisdom

BRING LIGHT INTO THE MIND,
UPLIFT YOUR HEART AND ACTIVATE
ENTHUSIASM AND DYNAMISM.
OVERCOME RESISTANCE TO FULLY
ENGAGING BY KINDLING THE INNER
FLAMES OF JOY AND PASSION.

GORSE
Ulex europaeus

JOY

The golden flowers of gorse are associated with intelligence, vibrancy and energy as they shine as brightly as the sun. The Druids recognised gorse as an exceptional light seeker.

Gorse flowers are bearers of light and joy. True joy is a sublime state of feeling yourself to be at peace with your true self. Through identification with this self, the life energies flow and radiate through the whole being, lighting up and uplifting body and mind, which vibrate with *joie de vivre.*

When the connection between these parts of your self are weakened by whatever cause – from stress, overload or despair, this joy of aliveness and wellbeing can go missing. Your consciousness may become clouded and a vague and dreamy state of indifference descends.

When darkness weighs down the mind and heart, gorse flower essence brings in the light of awareness and your connection with the joy of your true self. The movement of life force energises, strengthens and uplifts you, so that you are more enthusiastically engaged in life and in relating. From this unfaltering awareness comes new hope and the ability to appreciate and enjoy living every moment to the full.

- Dynamism and enthusiasm
- Uplift heart and mind
- Will and determination to stay mindful and connected
- Clarity of the connection with your vitality
- Strengthen your resolve
- Passionate engagement with life

INDICATIONS

- Lack of joy, passion or motivation
- Overly detached or withdrawn
- Downhearted or disheartened
- Repressed from apathy, defeatism or negativity
- Depleted energy, strength and willpower
- Holding back from real engagement in life

AFFIRMATION: I live my life with joy and passion.

CROSS REFERENCE

Alienation I Apathy I Awareness I Body I Darkness I Depression I Energy I Enthusiasm
Fatigue I Heartache I Hopelessness I Immunity I Insecurity I Joy I Lethargy I Life force
Light I Lightness I Motivation I Optimism I Passion I Relationship I Relaxation I Separation
Vitality I Winter blues

GRASS OF PARNASSUS

Parnassia palustris

OPENNESS

In the Ancient Greek pharmacopeia of the physician Dioscorides, widely read for more than 1500 years, he describes the medicinal properties of this plant, growing on Mount Parnassus, home of Apollo and the Muses.

Grass of Parnassus speaks to the soul whose heart is sensitive and vulnerable. Vulnerability is a doorway to open to love, and this flower teaches to you to "love like you've never been hurt". Real happiness comes when you give your love, and yourself, openly and freely.

A small child possesses the innate ability to spread loving kindness wherever it goes and to whomever it meets. When it is hurt it, it cries, and crying is a powerful tool for healing. But as we grow up we learn to avoid getting hurt, and to avoid crying, especially in public, which impedes the natural healing process.

You are put on guard and hold on to strategies designed to stop negative emotions from harming you. You try to protect yourself by containing experiences of pain and trauma, choosing to forget them until a time when you feel safe enough to heal. Suppression of feelings leads to emotional blockages while pushing the pain deeper inside.

Grass of Parnassus flower essence opens the heart to the healing power of love. When you have the courage to open your heart, to be more open and trusting, you radiate warm love and are sensitive to love in return.

- Connect more deeply with yourself and others
- Courage to live with an open heart
- Heal and transform the past
- Value and support your own vulnerability
- Emotional receptivity and sensitivity
- Embrace love, which provides heartfelt strength and protection

INDICATIONS

- Barriers to love
- Creating self-protective barriers to avoid feeling vulnerable
- Strenuously holding on to emotions of heartache and sadness
- Emotionally closed due to hurt in the past
- Hiding your real emotions
- Shutting down a part of yourself in self-defence and for protection

AFFIRMATION: I open my heart to let in love.
I feel and express my love in the world..

CROSS REFERENCE

Adolescence I Alienation I Aloofness I Birth and Birthing I Feminine principle I Fertility
Heartache I Inner child I Insecurity I Intimacy I Light I Loneliness I Love I Openness
Protection I Receptivity I Rejection I Relationship I Repression I Sadness I Security
Sensitivity I Soothing I Tenderness I Transformation I Trust I Vulnerability

BELIEVE IN YOURSELF. HAVE TRUST AND CONFIDENCE IN YOUR ABILITIES TO BE WELL AND PROSPER.

HAREBELL
Campanula rotundifolia

ALIGNMENT

Harebell is a medicinal herb that has been used for a variety of ailments, including depression. The flower is attributed with the qualities of delicacy and sweetness, and in the language of flowers with resignation, grief and submission.

You will attract into your life that which is in resonance with your thoughts and core beliefs ('energy follows thought'). Harebell flower essence can help you to align thoughts, words and actions that are in harmony with manifesting the success you desire in life.

Lack of trust, self-doubt and fear prejudice your ability to realise your potential and prosper. When you are in alignment with your true self that knows no limitations, by thinking and speaking with words that build confidence and keep you motivated towards achieving your goal, you begin to manifest positive results instead of dwelling on potential negative results.

When you have a strong belief in yourself and your abilities by drawing on and listening to your intuition, to the wisdom from deep inside yourself, you become the source of your own fulfilment, abundance and wellbeing.

ATTRIBUTES

Self-reliance and feeling secure in yourself

Live in the constant awareness that all is well in your world

Confidence in your creative abilities

Courage and conviction to embrace your highest path and purpose

Faith and trust in yourself

Listening to your inner voice to guide you in the right direction

INDICATIONS

Feelings of inadequacy

Negative self-talk

Lack of faith that prejudices your ability to realise your potential

Self-doubt and uncertainty; fear of failure

Taking the 'path of least resistance' as the easy choice

Not listening to and trusting your inner voice

AFFIRMATION: I align myself with the spirit of abundance
and have faith that all my needs are met.

CROSS REFERENCE

Alignment I Confidence I Courage I Decision I Faith I Goal I Grounding I Insecurity
Manifestation I Negativity I Optimism I Perseverance I Prosperity I Security I Self-
acceptance I Self-image I Self-love I Strength I Thinking/Thought patterns I Trust I Will

BE FREE TO 'GO WITH THE FLOW'
AND TRAVEL FORWARD IN WONDER
OF YOUR NEW UNFOLDING
POTENTIAL. TRANSFORM
EXPECTATIONS INTO EXPLORATIONS

HAZEL
Corylus avellana

FREEDOM

The virtues of the hazel are legendary. It is a tree associated with wisdom and is supposed to have the power to bestow knowledge, creativity and inspiration. Hazel opens the way to journey to the source from where creative energy springs forth.

People get attached to their thoughts and ideas, creating scenarios of how things should or should not be. Attachment to beliefs and attitudes creates much of the stress and anxiety that we feel in our lives. By thinking and acting on the basis of our expectations, we fall into the trap of trying to control the direction and flow of our lives. Expectation is the source of frustration that restricts our ability to open to new ideas and inspiration. When we transform our thinking about something, it transforms the way we feel about it.

The Buddha taught non-attachment as a way of liberation from suffering and a path to happiness. When life seems like a struggle and you are creatively stuck, hazel flower essence aids in releasing the sources of frustration and unhappiness by helping you to let go of expectations and patterns of thinking that cause doubt, fear and discontent. Focusing on the things you can control and releasing the things you can't brings inner peace and calm.

This essence gives you the freedom to explore new directions and to follow your inspiration. Tune into your inner wisdom source, allow yourself to just 'give up' and trust the way forward will be shown. Endeavour fearlessly and enjoy the sheer exhilaration of the journey!

- Let go and 'go with the flow'
- Transform expectations into explorations
- Let thoughts, ideas and inspiration flow naturally
- Surrender and trust as you follow the path unfolding before you
- Focus on where you want to go, relax and trust the process
- Willing openness and acceptance of the unfolding developments in your life

- Over-attachment to ideas, beliefs, thoughts
- Need to control, and be in control
- Holding on too tightly to expectations
- Repression of emotions
- Attachments to and difficulty breaking free from the past
- Restlessness without direction

AFFIRMATION: I travel forward in life with wonder and joy.

Action I Addiction I Birth and Birthing I Blocks I Breakthrough I Control I Flexibility
Freedom I Holding on I Non-attachment I Obstinate I Procrastination I Relaxation I Release
Rigidity I Resistance I Restlessness I Stagnation I Surrender I Thinking/Thought patterns
Transition I Trust

HOLY THORN
Crataegus

ACCEPTANCE

According to legend, the Glastonbury Thorn grew from a wooden staff said to have belonged to Jesus, when Joseph of Arimathea struck it into the ground. As well as flowering in spring, it flowers again at the Winter Solstice.

Hawthorn is an extremely valuable medicinal herb used mainly for treating disorders of the heart. The Holy Thorn symbolises acceptance and understanding extended from an open heart.

Holy Thorn flower essence brings gentleness to people who may have become hard-hearted, or who are hard on themselves and others. This creates barriers to being able to express yourself authentically in relationships. Whether from a need to protect your own heart from hurt, or from fear, it essentially blocks the flow of love that enables you to reach out, empathise and understand others' feelings and sentiments, and creates barriers to being able to express yourself genuinely in relationships.

The power of love is so great, it dissolves hurt, bitterness and all sense of injustice. When the heart *chakra* is awakened, the impulses of spiritual inspiration and altruistic love pour in and through you, allowing you to express yourself freely without fear.

By accepting yourself and others wholeheartedly and without reservation, you bare your heart and soul, the source of unconditional, transforming love. This manifests in your life as intuitiveness, deeper understanding and compassion; love-in-action that can transform suffering.

At its highest expression, this essence awakens you to the presence of universal Christ-like consciousness in yourself and in others. In the Buddhist tradition it expresses the Bodhisattva aspiration to assist all sentient beings to reach enlightenment.

ATTRIBUTES

Open your heart and let the true you speak out
Love and accept yourself and others unconditionally
Greater love and fellowship with others
Transformation and healing through the power of love
Reveal your true self through emotional connection and resonance
Be gentle and kind to yourself and others

INDICATIONS

Barriers to expressing love and affection
Self-critical awareness creating barriers to wholehearted communication
Being too hard on yourself and others
Old wounds and hurtful memories that close the heart
Self-sacrificing, and generally functioning independently of others
Over-detachment makes it difficult to connect with emotions

AFFIRMATION: I open my heart to feel and express love
and acceptance of myself, and others.

CROSS REFERENCE

Acceptance I Alienation I Aloofness I Altruism I Birth and Birthing I Blocks I Bonding
Compassion I Expression I Fertility I Forgiveness I Intolerance I Isolation I Love I Nurturing
Openness I Relationship I Rejection I Repression I Self-acceptance I Self-criticism I Self-
harm I Self-love I Sexuality I Tenderness I Tolerance I Unconditional love I Understanding

IONA PENNYWORT
Umbilicus rupestris

TRANSPARENCY

Pennywort is still used to treat a wide range of skin conditions and as a homeopathic remedy for ailments from suppressed emotions. This essence was prepared on the island of Iona.

Iona pennywort essence helps to penetrate the darkness by shining soul light on a problem that you are hiding, denying, or covering up. Light protects from darkness and also lets you see what is real and what is imaginary.

Personal weaknesses, shortcomings and instincts contained deep in the unconscious mind can be repressed and denied. Shame, guilt, self-judgment and 'beating yourself up' are consequences of denying the shadow side of yourself. The psychologist Carl Jung said, in relation to the shadow self, 'what you resist, persists'. His research revealed that whatever you are resisting about yourself takes energy and that constant resistance could fracture the psyche or ego.

Through conscious recognition of the 'shadow' parts of yourself you can recognise illusions the mind has created to avoid facing yourself truthfully. When the mind is caught up in illusion it can appear to be real, so illusion cannot be dispelled by the mind alone. This flower essence may help to bring in the light of awareness.

The discriminating mind conjoined with the soul's light of wisdom can dispel the fogs that cloud your consciousness. You realise that the darkness co-exists as part of the whole. The truth comes to light when light is shone on the truth.

- Bring in the light of self-conscious awareness
- Clear judgement and discernment
- Acknowledge and integrate all aspects of the self
- Truthfully face what you would rather avoid or ignore
- Accept and integrate your 'shadow' self
- Master your inner fears and demons

INDICATIONS

- Repressed, irrational fears
- Denial of your shadow side
- Fog of illusion between your psyche and the real world
- Repression of your shortcomings and weaknesses
- Fear that prevents you from seeing the truth
- Weaknesses and shortcomings hidden or denied

AFFIRMATION: I acknowledge and respect all aspects of myself. I am light.

CROSS REFERENCE

Addiction I Avoidance I Awareness I Darkness I Delusion I Denial I Discipline
Discrimination I Delusion I Dream and Dreaming I Fear I Grounding I Guilt I Habit patterns
Illusion I Integration I Judgemental I Light I Nightmare I Obsession I Polarity I Repression
Self-acceptance I Self-image I Self-sabotage I Shadow self I Shame I Unconscious mind

BRING TO LIGHT ALL YOUR INHERENT
POWER AND INTELLIGENCE. DISSIPATE
FALSE IMPRESSIONS IN AWARENESS
AND COGNITION BY BRIDGING THE
MIND-BODY CONNECTION.

LADY'S MANTLE
Alchemilla vulgaris

AWARENESS

Lady's Mantle's Latin name, *Alchemilla,* is derived from the ancient alchemists who prized the dew that collected in its leaves and they believed to have magical properties. It could be said that flower essences, in their method of preparation, are a simulation of the ancient alchemical art of dew collection.

This flower essence may help to strengthen the mind-body connection. By connecting rational and intuitive elements of the mind, we open doors into mindfulness. Through this unification we can realise deeper levels of awareness for optimal mental and physical performance.

Conscious awareness, comprehension and cognition may be limited or retarded when these connections are interrupted for any reason. This can be from stress or trauma, and also when traumatic memories buried in the unconscious are triggered in the conscious mind.

This essence can also help to access information from the unconscious, the part of the mind that receives and stores information, inspiration, and memories. It is helpful, for example, for remembering and understanding your dreams, as well as mastering the ability to organise yourself between left-brained and right-brained tasks.

Lady's Mantle flower essence may help to bring in presence of mind, and thereby more awareness, expanding your ability to focus and concentrate in the present moment. As understanding comes to the forefront of the mind, you respond intelligently in any situation and, rather than reacting, you can then take appropriate action.

- Secure mind-body connection for optimal mental and physical performance
- Integrate the rational and intuitive mind
- Expand mental awareness and responsiveness
- Wisdom through dreams and archetypes
- Enhance lateral thinking and problem solving
- Left and right brain collaboration assists creative reasoning faculties

INDICATIONS
- Lack of co-ordination affecting your thinking and comprehension
- Impaired powers of deciphering and processing information
- Loosening of connection between mental and emotional bodies
- Diminished awareness from dissociation of logic and reasoning faculties
- Slow response to stimulus
- Polarisation of reasoning faculties and 'common' sense

AFFIRMATION I bring to light all the wisdom and awareness I need.

CROSS REFERENCE
Apathy I Attention I Awareness I Communication I Comprehension I Confusion I Dream and Dreaming I Focus I Insecurity I Integration I Knowledge I Learning I Light I Memory Nightmare I Out-of-body I Overwhelm I Perception I Polarity I Sensitivity I Sleep patterns Speaking I Understanding I Unconscious mind

HOLD YOUR VISION, GET
ORGANISED AND BRING YOUR
PLAN INTO MANIFESTATION.

LAUREL
Prunus lusitanica

RESOURCEFULNESS

Garlands of laurel, as symbols of excellence and victory, were used to crown poets, musicians, and athletes at the first Olympic games. This custom endures in expressions such as Nobel laureate. The priestesses of Delphi used laurel to enhance their prophetic abilities.

Laurel flower essence can help to synthesise and harmonise different aspects of the mind: the concrete, reasoning mind and the intuitive abstract mind, and thereby bring order into your thinking processes.

Manifesting anything takes energy and vision. If your attention is fragmented, moving from one thought to another, you are not able to hold a clear vision of a plan of action. Without a plan, your goal has little chance of success. To bring inspiration, the 'vision' of the plan, down from the world of ideas to the level of recognition and understanding, the brain must register the abstract idea before the mind can interpret it.

Laurel flower essence helps to organise, direct, plan and structure your thoughts in line with your intention. Inspired with the idea and formulating a clear and concise mental picture and vision of exactly what you want, and by your intention, your highest dreams become a reality.

ATTRIBUTES

» Bring ideas into being and put them into action
» Form a clear mental picture and vision of exactly what you want to manifest
» Synthesise and organise different facets of a plan into a unified whole
» Develop the ability to have a single-pointed focus
» Setting goals and priorities
» Commitment to follow the path you have chosen

INDICATIONS

» Depletion of mental focus and energy through lack of one-pointed focus
» Disorganised mind leads to ineffective thought-form building
» Not focusing on the next thing to be achieved
» Failure to follow through when you lose sight of your vision
» Scattered and fragmented thinking obscures ability to hold a clear vision
» Drifting aimlessly without following the path you have chosen

AFFIRMATION: I manifest all that I need to fulfil the Divine Plan.
I work for the good of the whole.

CROSS REFERENCE

Action | Awareness | Clarity | Commitment | Discrimination | Empowerment | Focus
Goal | Inspiration | Intuition | Leadership | Manifestation | Motivation | Perseverance
Procrastination | Prosperity | Purpose | Responsibility | Self-sabotage | Thinking/Thought
patterns | Vision | Will | Wisdom

LIME
Tilia platyphyllos

UNIVERSALITY

The lime tree has been praised in history and folklore across Europe for centuries and continues to be valued for its medicinal properties. Symbolically, it is associated with comfort, friendship, love and protection and was also believed to inspire fairness and justice.

Lime cultivates peace and harmony in the heart and mind. It teaches that inner peace exists within you right now and can be accessed when you choose to accept things as they are. Peace in the outer world arrives when we make peace with ourselves.

Harbouring negative thoughts or energies creates disharmony between your heart and mind. A negative attitude drains your energy, increases negative thinking habits and can dispose you to reactionary behaviour. Exercising tolerance is difficult when you feel inadequate, insecure and ineffective. These deep-seated habits result from a sense of separation from self and others and ultimately the inability to love yourself and to receive love from others.

The illusion of being separate from those around us arises when we distinguish between self and others and identify with the differences. The inner conflict of feeling 'separate' is healed by unconditional love that allows peace to blossom from within. We rise above the dichotomy of separation and, through unification with the soul, our true self. This brings greater awareness of self in relationship to everything.

The realisation of oneness is achieved from a place of unity within, when we open our hearts to the light and love of our universal being, and thereby the ability to love and be loved. Love is interconnectedness, relatedness and oneness.

The realisation of oneness is the goal of all true spiritual practices. We develop universal love and compassion through harmlessness and selfless service to others, by doing the most loving thing in each situation, letting love determine the way.

Acceptance of yourself and others beyond differences

Healing the heart and soul from the pain of separation

Realisation of inner reconciliation of self with the whole

Restore inner peace in spite of outer circumstances

Self-responsibility and group awareness

Patient tolerance, self-control, and sensitivity

INDICATIONS

Over-identification with the ego that polarises and separates

Inner turmoil and dissonance leading to feelings of powerlessness

Separative and unmindful attitudes and behaviour

Feelings of alienation and loneliness

Inner turmoil that creates dissonance

Harbouring grudges for imagined wrongs

AFFIRMATION I open my heart to create harmonious relationships in life.
I am one with all other beings.

CROSS REFERENCE

Acceptance I Alienation I Compassion I Criticism I Defensiveness I Discrimination
Hostility I Insecurity I Intolerance I Irritability I Judgemental I Negativity I Openness
Peace I Reconciliation I Relationship I Responsibility I Rigidity I Separation I Self-love
Thinking/Thought patterns I Tolerance I Unconditional love

UNITE THINKING WITH FEELING BY
ACCESSING THE WISDOM OF YOUR
TRUE SELF. THINK AND COMMUNICATE
FROM THE HEART.

MALLOW
Malva sylvestris

GRACE

Mallow has been valued as a medicine since ancient times and was believed to be a cure-all. The meaning given in the language of flowers is beneficence and kindness. According to mythology, mallows were the first gift sent to earth by the gods to prove that they had humanity's best interests at heart.

Creative thought and inspiration flow from the unity of body and soul, mind and heart. From this alignment the wisdom of the heart, the inherent wisdom of your true self manifests through thought, words and actions.

When you are overly detached from your feelings or preoccupied with your own thoughts, you can get stuck in your thinking pattern and hardened in your feelings. There is no separation between thought and feeling for they ultimately exist in a continuum. Mallow flower essence helps to bridge the polarities between thought and feeling.

You can hear the purity in a person's heart as they vocalise. When you resonate with the clear note that is sounded by the soul, it resounds through the heart and mind. Mallow flower essence helps you to think with your heart.

A divine idea or high ideal may then be realised and expressed with heartfelt meaning, reflecting the purpose perfectly and in accordance with your intention. This is grace, and grace can be defined as your divine nature in action.

- Practical, concrete expression and application of thoughts and ideas
- Harmonise thinking with feeling
- Reason and intuition working together
- Clear and heartfelt communication
- Flow of creative life energy through the heart
- Ability to discern and express 'the good, the true and the beautiful'

INDICATIONS

- Detachment of thinking and feeling functions
- Awkwardness when expressing your feelings in words
- Indecisive vacillation from over-analysis of all options and sides
- Over-intellectualising rather than expressing your feelings
- Abandonment of the intuition and relying solely on reason and logic
- Fixed ideas overpowering creativity

AFFIRMATION: I harmonise love and will. I speak and act from the heart.

CROSS REFERENCE

Attunement I Awareness I Clarity I Communication I Decision I Intuition I Male/Female balance I Polarity I Receptivity I Reconciliation I Relationship I Separation I Speaking Thinking/Thought patterns I Wisdom I Writing

MONKEY FLOWER
Mimulus guttatus

PERSONAL POWER

Monkey flower became a symbol of humour, perhaps because the flowers resemble a monkey's face. Native peoples used the plant mostly for healing wounds. Mimulus was prepared by Dr Edward Bach and is prescribed for 'fear or anxiety of known origin'.

This flower essence helps to raise your vibrational energy from the personality to the higher self. The process of lifting your energies from being focused in the solar plexus *chakra* (the centre that processes emotions) to the heart *chakra* (the centre of unconditional love and awareness) calms the emotional body by bringing the love and strength of the higher to the lower self.

Monkey flower helps to transform and transmute fears held in the unconscious mind that limit your personal power in the world. The soul needing this essence may be very sensitive and withdraw from stress or conflict as a means of self-protection. This is a common defence mechanism, to withdraw rather than face possible confrontation and so block the threat of pain and being hurt.

When you are centred within yourself, in the heart, there is no need to cover up your vulnerability or fear. The sense of security that arises when you stand in your power gives you confidence to face any challenge head-on.

ATTRIBUTES

- Acting from strength of individual purpose
- Courage to face and transcend your fears
- Maintain personal boundaries
- Take charge of your negative emotions and reactions
- Bring the strength of the higher self to personality expression
- Face your fears in the light of understanding

INDICATIONS

- Over-sensitive and submissive when not standing in your power
- Highly reactive from fear of being overpowered
- Apprehension leads to disempowerment
- Withdraw from challenges and give in to fear
- Easily intimidated, lack of confidence
- Fear of feeling helpless from stress or during a conflict

AFFIRMATION I celebrate who I am. I stand in my uniqueness and truth to serve all.

CROSS REFERENCE

Anger I Anxiety I Assertiveness I Bullying I Confidence I Courage I Expression I Fear
Higher self I Inferiority I Inner child I Insecurity I Irritability I Nervousness I Purpose
Repression I Self-acceptance I Self-esteem I Shyness I Victim

RAGGED ROBIN
Lychnis flos-cuculi

PURIFICATION

Ragged robin loves to grow in damp places. The roots contain saponins that were used as a soap substitute. In the language of flowers ragged robin is a symbol of ardour and 'keeping your wits about you'.

As a flower essence, it helps to purify the blockages within your subtle energy channels that cause friction and an irregular flow of life force. Suppressed emotions, fixed ideas and rigid thinking all contribute to creating obstacles that impede your energy flow. These may become harmful and give rise to weakness in one or more of the subtle bodies, thereby affecting general health and wellbeing. Detoxification and purification are fundamental therapies used in traditional holistic mind-body healing systems. Self-discipline - in some form and to some degree - is an important part of spiritual practice, characterised by the longing to free yourself from habitual patterns and desires that may be in control in a variety of ways in your life. However, it is important to maintain balance and not swing to the opposite pole by adopting the mindset that rejects pleasurable or worldly things as bad for the soul.

Ragged robin flower essence may help to remove the obstacles that cloud your perception of what is good for you and what is not, so that you can consciously choose what you eliminate, absorb, and transmit in your life with the highest respect for the sanctity of your mind-body's integrity and wholeness. Then, choices that affirm the soul's attributes are strengthened and embodied.

Purify your energy channels (*nadi*)

Clear your mental and emotional fields to allow thoughts and feelings to flow

Discernment and clarity of what is good for you and what is not

Consciously choose what you absorb, eliminate and transmit in your life

Make conscious choices that strengthen the embodiment of soul attributes

Cultivate a way of life that attunes you to the inner self

INDICATIONS

Blocks that impede your energy flow

Toxic thoughts and repressed emotions that inhibit soul expression

Obstacles to soul growth and transformation

Self-punishing attitudes/behaviour

Blockages within the subtle energy channels that cause friction,
and irregular flow of life force

Fixed ideas about what is good for you and what is not

AFFIRMATION: I purify myself and clear my channels.
My energies flow free and I am restored to wholeness.

CROSS REFERENCE

Blocks | Body | Catharsis | Desire | Discipline | Discrimination | Flexibility | Habit patterns
Life force | Obsession | Perfectionism | Release | Repression | Rigidity | Self-criticism
Self-harm | Self-image | Self-pity | Resistance | Thinking/Thought patterns

REINDEER LICHEN
Cladonia mitis

TRANSMUTATION

Lichens consist of two different organisms, a fungus and an alga that live together symbiotically. Many lichens are known to be very sensitive to environmental pollution and they have been used as 'indicator' species. Reindeer lichens are able to take up moisture from the air. It was reported that indigenous Aleut hunters of Alaska drank it as a tea to 'maintain their wind' when climbing in the hills.

Breath is *prana* and the fluid of connection that controls the breathing process. Breathing is the alchemy of the absorption of air and its transmutation into *prana* or life force, which revitalises every part of the body. We breathe the external world within, and through the breath we become conscious in our relationship to the environment.

When the heart is afflicted by grief or loss, the heart *chakra* is affected and the etheric channels that convey the life force can become restricted or blocked. Reindeer lichen essence revitalises the etheric heart centre. This *chakra* that transforms and transmutes, when awakened, the emotions of the solar plexus *chakra* into love energy by clearing congestion.

We are conscious that suffering is inherently part of the human experience of being in physical form. By accepting the concept of 'impermanence' with patient understanding, you can surrender suffering as part of the soul's plan for the evolution of growth, adaptation and self-realisation.

By opening to the power of love, you can purify, transform and transmute suffering. You breathe in peace and you breathe out peace when you find your centre of balance in the heart.

Graceful flow of heart and soul energy, the energy of love

Using breath for the purposes of transmuting and shifting energies

The alchemy of converting solar *prana* to vital energy

Accept all emotions as sacred; feel the pain and let go

Live and love without limits

Breathe, relax and calm the heart and mind

Repressed emotions that inhibit the flow of life force

Fear inhibits feeling strong emotions

Not allowing the energy to move in your life

Heart contracts in the face of pain and suffering

Grief and loss held in the heart

Withdrawal and not embracing life fully

AFFIRMATION: I purify myself and allow love to flow in and through me.

Alienation ∣ Blocks ∣ Body ∣ Forgiveness ∣ Grief ∣ Heartache ∣ Hopelessness ∣ Integration Life force ∣ Loss ∣ Pain ∣ Pining ∣ Relationship ∣ Release ∣ Repression ∣ Sadness ∣ Self-realisation ∣ Surrender ∣ Transformation

ROSE ALBA
Rosa alba

POWER

Since time immemorial the world has eulogised the rose as the flower of love. The Jacobite rose, the wild rose of Scotland, represents reverence, worthiness, purity and loyalty.

Rose Alba flower essence represents the vital, creative principle of power. This is the positive, 'yang' principle that initiates and purposefully calls on and applies the inner driving force or impetus to activate, build and create. The essence stands for the right use of this power.

Power needs to be wielded wisely and with love. When not balanced with love, power can be destructive and lead to abuse. Rose Alba flower essence connects you to the source of your true power, your higher self, so that you are able to bring in the higher aspect of will and purpose, and harmonise it with intuitive love and wisdom. Your intuition is never wrong, although your interpretation of it may be imperfect. Awareness is key to help you accurately understand and respond to intuition.

When you are connected to your higher self, your intuition can speak to you. It takes patience, persistence and perseverance to keep this connection. Effort and endeavour are an integral part of setting the creative forces in motion.

You can then channel your creative powers in the most appropriate ways, acting spontaneously and trusting your intuitive knowledge. When you trust and follow your intuition, right speech and right action follow.

ATTRIBUTES

Connecting lower and higher mind

Impeccability of action guided by your intuition

Connect with your true inner authority and 'walk your talk'

Channel creative power through words and action

Enlightened power and leadership

Will-directed consciousness

INDICATIONS

Out of alignment with your inner power and authority

Obstacles to putting your thoughts and ideas into words and action

Not acting on messages from your body, heart and soul

Rigid thinking and over-rationalisation blocks the flow of inspiration

Issues with authority or the father or masculine principle

Misuse of personal willpower

AFFIRMATION: I align myself with Divine Will. I am love in action.

CROSS REFERENCE

Action ǀ Alignment ǀ Assertivness ǀ Attunement ǀ Channelling ǀ Communication ǀ Creativity Discipline ǀ Empowerment ǀ Expression ǀ Flexibility ǀ Higher self ǀ Inspiration ǀ Intuition Leadership ǀ Masculine principle ǀ Patience ǀ Perseverance ǀ Power ǀ Purpose Responsibility ǀ Rigidity ǀ Sexuality ǀ Speaking ǀ Will ǀ Writing

ROSE WATER LILY
Nymphaea

PRESENCE

In Hinduism and Buddhism the lotus flower has become a symbol for awakening to the spiritual reality of life. It is symbolic of rebirth because it opens to the sun and closes at sunset. Emerging from the depths of the muddy waters into the clear light, the lily is a symbol of the interconnectedness and interdependence of spirit and matter.

Rose Water Lily flower essence represents the parallels between the spiritual and physical worlds and reminds us that the unfoldment of our divine potential is inherent, and our birthright.

When you get caught up in the commotion and the drama of your life, you can become disconnected from your spiritual self, metaphorically lose your way, your devotion to your purpose, and become dreamy and ungrounded. This can leave you feeling bereft, alone and yearning for harmony and meaning in your life.

Rose Water Lily flower essence can help to cultivate your awareness to stay present in the moment, to rise above the pressures and demands of daily living and to realise that, with regard to personal suffering, "this too shall pass". In the company and presence of the true self, there is serenity and peace and deep, abiding trust.

ATTRIBUTES

Inner strength and courage when you feel disheartened
Lift your consciousness and your spirits
Uniting inner and outer paths through spiritual emergence
Regain emotional tranquillity and contentment
Feel more connected and at home in the physical world
Connection with your spiritual roots and creative source

INDICATIONS

Caught up in the stresses of personal dramas
Disheartened with the mundane and habitual
Emotionally restless and discontent
Yearning for connection and a sense of higher purpose
Disorientation, the sense that one is 'off course'
Feelings of loneliness or isolation in your plight

AFFIRMATION Pure in heart and in truth I stand. I AM.

CROSS REFERENCE

Abandonment ı Alienation ı Anxiety ı Blocks ı Calm ı Courage ı Darkness ı Death and Dying ı Despair ı Faith ı Grounding ı Heartache ı Higher ı Self ı Light ı Loneliness ı Loss Love ı Out-of-body ı Peace ı Pining ı Restlessness ı Sadness ı Separation ı Spiritual connection ı Spiritual emergence ı Strength ı Stress ı Surrender

ROWAN
Sorbus aucuparia

RECONCILIATION

Rowan is steeped in history and is still seen and used today as a tree of vision, healing and communication. It symbolises growth and rebirth and its message is right discrimination in what you hold fast to and what you let go of.

Its message is to accept and take responsibility for having co-created a situation with others for some purpose that your soul and higher self knows, and to honour how your experiences and actions have engendered who you are today.

Rowan flower essence helps to focus on what we have done in order to learn from the experience. In some instances, this may mean reaching back into the past to process events and repair relationships and that caused pain or suffering.

Harbouring feelings of anger, bitterness and resentment armours the heart with defensiveness, drains your energy and reduces the level of your vitality. Negative emotions that are not resolved can manifest again in other situations and relationships that have nothing to do with the original trauma.

Our spiritual work in healing and releasing past traumas allows the lesson to unfold, while monitoring our behaviour and responses to them, in order to learn our lessons from these situations. This essence helps you to recognise that this isn't the same lesson repeating itself but is a deeper level of soul work, as you honour the work that has already been done and acknowledge it as the foundation for the next level of learning. Often the best decision is to simply let the pain go, get over it and move on with your life. To forgive means 'to give up' and forgiveness is the single most important practice that brings peace to our souls and harmony to our lives. As we reach out to the ones who hurt us, we are the ones who heal.

- Seize opportunities that bring harmony and healing potential
- Take responsible action to resolve problems and misunderstandings
- Wisdom that clears the way to releasing karmic complexes held in the subtle bodies
- Discrimination of what to let go of that is harmful and what to hold on to that is beneficial
- Bring care and understanding into your relationships
- Acknowledge responsibility for healing the cause of past suffering

INDICATIONS

- Strained relations due to unresolved problems and misunderstandings
- Patterns of behaviour that cause friction in relationships
- Negative karmic complexes held in the subtle bodies
- Injury that has toughened your heart
- Reduced capacity to connect with people who have hurt you in the past
- Let go of resentment and end estrangement

AFFIRMATION: I experience forgiveness of myself and others, and surrender to unconditional healing love.

CROSS REFERENCE

Acceptance I Anger I Blame I Blocks I Bullying I Conflict I Defensiveness I Forgiveness
Grief I Hostility I Irritability I Judgemental I Karma I Negativity I Pain I Reconciliation
Relationship I Release I Repression I Resentment I Rigidity I Self-pity I Shame I Tension
Tolerance I Victim I Understanding I Unconditional love

TRUST THE SOURCE OF WISDOM WITHIN YOU. OVERCOME THE INSECURITY OF UNCERTAINTY BY TUNING IN AND LISTENING. BE GUIDED BY YOUR INNER VOICE.

SCOTS PINE
Pinus sylvestris

WISDOM

The Scots pine made up most of the ancient Caledonian forest and symbolises in-stinctual wisdom. It was considered the 'king of the forest', the tree of heroes, chief-tains and warriors. Scots pine has been used as a medicinal plant for many centuries. Scots Pine flower essence helps to access the source of wisdom and knowing from within the self and supports you in finding confidence in trusting the choices and decisions you make, and the directions you take in life.

The person who is insecure may lack confidence and doubt their abilities due to a negative perception of their own value and capability. Setting very high standards of performance for yourself, whether from being perfectionist, or from an inner drive for approval, may lead to self-blame from the judgement that you are not fulfilling your own high ideals. Doubt and lack of trust fuels the perceived sense of your inadequacy.

When you connect with the wisdom of your true self, you automatically trust your inner knowing and consequently realise what the next step to be taken is. Then you can affirm, in all confidence, that you have the all the power and intelligence that you need within you.

ATTRIBUTES

- Trust your inner knowing
- Faith and confidence in your powers of discernment and understanding
- Accept yourself and trust your actions
- Strength of character and certainty within the self
- Lighten up and be kind to yourself
- Set realistic goals for yourself with more calmness and objectivity

INDICATIONS

- Over-dependence on outside validation and reassurance
- Not trusting yourself to make good choices and decisions
- Insecurity from a sense of inadequacy
- Self-doubt and blame
- Fear of making mistakes delays decision-making capacities
- Over-conscientiousness that leads to over-striving

AFFIRMATION I am receptive to the truth and wisdom within my being

CROSS REFERENCE

Assertiveness I Blame I Centering I Channelling I Clarity I Confidence I Confusion
Decision I Discrimination I Empowerment I Guilt I Insecurity I Intuition I Perfectionism
Self-criticism I Self-esteem I Self-love I Thinking/Thought patterns I Trust
Understanding I Universal mind I Wisdom I Worry

FIND INNER PEACE AND RESTORE
NATURAL RHYTHMS. OVERCOME
CONFLICT, FEAR AND ANXIETY BY
OPENING THE HEART TO THE SOURCE
OF UNCONDITIONAL, UNIVERSAL LOVE.

SCOTTISH PRIMROSE
Primula scotica

PEACE

Scottish primrose is a species of primrose that is endemic to the north coast of
Scotland, closely related to the Arctic species. It is regarded by botanists as one
of the most scarce and attractive plants in the world. This flower is the jewel in the
heart of the Findhorn Flower Essence range because it cultivates inner peace of
mind, heart and soul.

The greatest challenge for anyone who is attempting to cultivate a calm mentality
is to become free from negative emotions such as anxiety and fear. For this reason,
accessing true peace of mind is vital in achieving a disposition that is free from
stress and conflict.

One has to cultivate inner peace first, where it can gradually expand out like a
ripple effect into one's family unit, circle of friends, wider community, and ultimately the planet as a whole. This essence supports inner serenity by relaxing and
by opening the heart to the expansive experience and flow of unconditional love.
Scottish primrose moves us into a state of loving tenderness, enlightened understanding and compassion, and when this inner peace ultimately radiates out into
the collective consciousness, true peace can be realised.

- Peace of mind, serenity and calmness
- Balanced natural rhythms and equilibrium
- Grounded, connected and centred
- Relax, release and unwind
- Opening your heart to the expansive experience and flow of unconditional love
- Knowing and understanding that keeps you strong in the face of conflict

INDICATIONS

- Stress, agitation or inner conflict
- Friction that produces heartfelt distress
- Trauma from life changes and transformation
- Aftermath of shock; etheric and astral body cleavage
- Grief and heartache
- Not grounded in the body

AFFIRMATION: I am at peace in my heart and in the world.

CROSS REFERENCE

Anxiety I Body I Calm I Centering I Compassion I Conflict I Crisis I Emergency I Fear
Grief I Grounding I Heartache I Love I Nervousness I Out-of-body I Pain I Panic I Peace
Reconciliation I Relationship I Relaxation I Separation I Shock I Sleep patterns I Soothing
Tension I Trauma I Understanding I Unconditional love

SEA HOLLY
Eryngium maritimum

BRILLIANCE

Sea holly roots were collected on a large scale in the 17th and 18th centuries in England and were candied, then used as restorative, quasi-aphrodisiac lozenges. The language of flowers meaning is 'attractiveness'. Sea holly has sharp, prickly leaves that protect the tender heart of the flower. With Sea holly essence we are able to let down barriers of self-protection and foster a calm and concentrated inner peace by overcoming our insecurities and inhibitions.

The sensitive soul may armour itself against being vulnerable to criticism, from looking foolish and, in the extreme, from rejection. Many of us have suffered from feelings of self-consciousness or nervousness in public; there is motivation to make a desired impression along with doubt about having the ability to do so. Fear of saying or doing the wrong thing or of making a mistake can cause negative self-talk that inhibits self-expression and creates barriers in relating.

Sea holly flower essence helps you to step out boldly and to express your thoughts, feelings and ideas with confidence. You feel truly liberated when you open up to re-alising your full potential, standing in your power to be the radiant, enterprising and brilliant being that you are.

- Express yourself with calm, concentrated confidence
- Let your inner light and beauty shine
- Spontaneous, social and outgoing
- Be open and realise there are no limitations to expressing yourself
- Self-assured and composed so you can make the desired impression
- Let down self-protective barriers

INDICATIONS

- High personal performance standards
- Insecurities that inhibit your expression
- Uneasiness from fear of being judged negatively
- Worry about making the wrong impression
- Overly self-conscious
- Armouring yourself against criticism or looking foolish

AFFIRMATION: I am bold and fearless. I let my inner light shine.

CROSS REFERENCE

Aloofness | Anxiety | Blocks | Bullying | Communication | Confidence | Courage | Criticism
Creativity | Empowerment | Expression | Inferiority | Inner child | Insecurity | Nervousness
Openness | Rejection | Relationship | Repression | Self-empowerment | Self-image
Sensitivity | Shame | Shyness | Speaking | Trust | Vulnerability

SEA PINK
Armeria maritima

HARMONY

According to folklore, you will always thrive if you have sea pink growing in your garden. Dr Edward Bach, the modern founder of flower essences, imparted the truth that all disease is the result of disharmony or friction between the will of the soul, as a centre of consciousness, and the will of the personality, as a centre of experience. The body, mind, emotions and spirit are dynamically interrelated and each time a change is introduced at one level, it has a ripple effect throughout the entire system. Sea pink flower essence addresses the problems of division or cleavage. Separation can occur between the inner polarities (thought from feeling, for example), between the personality bodies – physical, emotional, mental and spiritual – or between different parts of the self, such as sub-personalities. As the physical and sentient nature responds to desire, you can vacillate between the pairs of opposites and feel fragmented, ungrounded and disconnected.
Sea pink may also help to release energetic blocks within the etheric and subtle bodies, helping to achieve a dynamic balance of the energy-distribution system as a whole. Integrated functioning of the mind: the mental body, and the sentient astral body, with the physical/etheric body, contributes to a greater integration between them, and with the soul body. When the life force emanations precipitate into the etheric body and circulate freely, the physical body remains in a vitalised condition. The inner dualities of body and soul, form and consciousness can thereby come into a more balanced state of being, where they mutually interpenetrate and work together in harmony.

ATTRIBUTES

- Clear, balance and harmonise your energies to optimise flow of life force
- Honouring and getting into a different relationship with all energies within you
- Working with heart, body, mind and energy consciously
- Balance and integrate your inner opposing forces
- Bring to light those parts of yourself which are the cause of your behaviour and feelings
- Owning your disavowed parts and integrating the inner polarities

INDICATIONS

- Disconnected and ungrounded
- Inner opposing forces in conflict with each other
- Splits in the psyche
- 'Divided against ourselves'
- Spacey, disoriented and not grounded
- Vacillation between opposite points of view

AFFIRMATION: I unify all energies within my being and welcome the balance and harmony.

CROSS REFERENCE

Awareness I Blocks I Centering I Confusion I Desire I Energy I Grounding I Integration Life force I Overwhelm I Polarity I Receptivity I Relationship I Separation I Sexuality Thinking/Thought patterns I Vitality

USE YOUR RESOURCES WISELY.
RELEASE INSECURITY AND THE
DESIRE TO HOLD ON. CONNECT TO
YOUR SOURCE, AND TRUST IN YOUR
POWERS TO ADAPT AND THRIVE.

SEA ROCKET
Cakile maritima

HARMONY

Sea rocket is a salt-tolerant beach plant. Its floating saltwater-resistant seedpod assures its survival. The message of sea rocket is tied in with the message and symbolism of the element of water. Water flows by conforming to the requirements of the environment and can change its course at a moment's notice. Sea rocket's message is to allow our emotions to adapt in balance and harmony to the currents of life.

Life often places many demands on us. Work-life balance is a fine line between meeting those demands and responsibilities, and feeling overloaded or stressed. Stress is the body's way of responding to any demand, but if the pressure becomes too great you can become overwhelmed. You may feel powerless in being able to create what you want and overcompensate, looking outside of yourself for creative solutions. As your focus and attention becomes dispersed, a flood of emotions in response to stress-related influences may make you feel as though your body, mind and emotions are out of control.

Sea rocket flower essence helps you to recognise that you have an innate capability to adapt to changing circumstances and environments, and this adaptability is an inherent power of the creative force. Instead of being tossed back and forth by the waves of circumstance, sea rocket helps you to be aware of and responsive to your own needs, to know that you have within you the resources to meet the need and to make the most of what you have been given.

By welcoming and allowing the abundant flow of life energy through every part of your being you can achieve greater mental and emotional stability. Trusting that all needs can, and will, be perfectly met is the natural outcome.

Be flexible and maximise functioning

Make the most of available resources in the situation you are facing

Adapt to change, succeed and flourish

Balance of holding on and letting go

Inner security, stability and constancy

Helping build a sense of self that's resilient and strong

INDICATIONS

Insecurity creates the need to hold on to control

Overcompensation, dominance and over striving

Changeable, unpredictable, fluctuating moods

Energy retention and congestion leading to depletion

Self-devaluation when you don't meet up to your own expectations

Easily overwhelmed by your responsibilities

AFFIRMATION: I trust in universal abundance. I give and receive freely.

CROSS REFERENCE

Change | Clarity | Control | Creativity | Discipline | Energy | Faith | Feminine principle
Fertility | Habit patterns | Holding on | Insecurity | Manifestation | Materialism | Mood swing
Nurturing | Perseverance | Prosperity | Rejuvenation | Security | Separation | Shadow self
Trust | Victim

SILVERWEED
Potentilla anserina

SIMPLICITY

The five-petalled yellow flower of *Potentilla* was a motif used by medieval knights who had achieved mastery over the self. The language of flowers lists the meaning of silverweed as naïveté. Silverweed teaches the merit of cultivating behaviour and habits that promote balanced living in harmony with yourself and nature.

As the lower personality seeks security, stability and the love of earthly things, it is a natural human trait to seek beauty and thereby find satisfaction in the gratification of your desires, pleasures and appetites. Silverweed flower essence is helpful when you become too identified with the physical being at the expense of your true self. When you become overly identified with the material world, you may lose contact with your purpose and intention. Over-identification with the form level of being may lead to excesses, instinctual drives, desires and behaviours that are not beneficial to personal harmony and wellbeing.

Silverweed essence supports mastery by enhancing self-realisation that leads to new ways of understanding and being. By non-attachment to the fascinations of the lower self, you realise that virtue and beauty is expressed on the 'golden mean' between the extremes, between needs and wants, sufficiency and deficiency.

The ability to let go and be non-attached is the way to happiness, according to the Buddha. Silverweed flower essence promotes vital enjoyment of, and interest in, the beauty of the simple things in life.

- Simplify your life in order to focus on things that are most important
- Voluntary practices to simplify your lifestyle
- Avoidance of excesses or extremes
- Adopt a calm composure, command your impulses and master your behaviour
- Heightened awareness of your attachments
- Enlightened self-interest based on a prudent understanding

INDICATIONS

- Out of control, impelling or irrepressible impulses and desires
- Seeking fulfilment through gratification of the sense pleasures
- Emotionally attached to material things
- Attachments that are obstacles to a serene and fulfilled life
- Preoccupied with incidentals; finicky and pernickety
- Excessive desire to consume and acquire material goods

AFFIRMATION: I live lightly on the earth and treasure all of nature's gifts.

CROSS REFERENCE

Addiction I Calm I Desire I Discipline I Grounding I Habit patterns I Holding on I Lightness
Materialism I Non-attachment I Obsession I Obstinate I Perfectionism I Release I Rigidity
Self-realisation I Thinking/Thought patterns I Trust

SNOWDROP
Galanthus nivalis

SURRENDER

Snowdrop is regarded as the first flower of spring in the Northern hemisphere and symbolises purity and the cleansing of the earth after winter. This flower symbolises moving from darkness to light. Like the phoenix of immortality rising from the ashes of the old, snowdrops burst into the world, their warmth melting ice and snow. Snowdrop flower essence helps us to triumph over fear, grief and pain, particularly in times of change and transition. When we accept our powerlessness over circumstances that cannot be controlled or changed, we reach a turning point. Snowdrop shows us that there is no holding back the tide so we may as well flow with it, even if it is not easy or comfortable.

When we surrender our attachments to the past, and to what is passing, we find freedom and new hope. Like the light at the end of the tunnel, a clear vision of the future may be revealed in all its beauty and potential, as we consciously move towards that vision with renewed hope and optimism.

ATTRIBUTES

ATTRIBUTES

Peaceful surrender by adapting to life changes and transitions

Release and let go of the past and what is passing

Optimism and hope for the future

Inner radiance in times of darkness

Serenity and peace through acceptance

Break through to new levels of awareness and understanding

INDICATIONS

Feelings of hopelessness; doom and gloom

Resistance to change

Grief, sorrow and loss

Frozen emotions

Fear of change and the unknown

Fear of letting go of someone or something

AFFIRMATION: I surrender and release that which has passed
and rejoice in the coming of the new.

CROSS REFERENCE

Acceptance I Addiction I Alienation I Blocks I Breakthrough I Change I Darkness
Death and Dying I Depression I Despair I Grief I Hopelessness I Light I Lightness I Loss
Negativity I Nightmare I Non-attachment I Optimism I Pain I Pining I Release I Resistance
Sadness I Separation I Strength I Surrender I Transition I Trust I Winter blues

BE POSITIVE. SURRENDER YOUR
LIMITED VIEWPOINT AND KEEP
THE GREATER PLAN IN MIND.

SPOTTED ORCHID
Dactylorhiza fuchsii

EQUANIMITY

Orchids are a symbol of perfection and beauty. Spotted orchid flowers display their beauty in minute, exquisite detail. This flower essence is beneficial when there is a tendency to get caught up in the minutiae – the small and precise details of something – and lose sight of the bigger picture.

The soul in need of spotted orchid may be perfectionistic, impulsive and attentionally 'short sighted'. With critical and meticulous attention to detail, they strain compulsively and unremittingly towards their goal. Personal success is measured in terms of productivity and accomplishment. This can be a form of over-compensation, where real or imagined weaknesses, frustrations, or feelings of inadequacy are consciously or unconsciously concealed by striving for excellence in another life area.

Spotted orchid flower essence helps to bring balance through self-regulation. Harnessing your willpower, and managing inner impulses and drives, allows you to focus on your greater mission or plan, to rise above narrow views or self-interest and to look beyond perceived imperfections.

When you can stand back and observe with broader vision and a fresh, more positive attitude, imaginative and creative solutions emerge that bring the sought after reward of personal acceptance, fulfillment and contentment.

Optimistic, broadminded, creative thinking
See the 'bigger picture' and align everything you do to that
Motivated by inspiration rather than compulsion
Calmness in decision making and problem solving
Self-regulatory effort and sacrifice to avoid temptation
Acceptance of yourself and others as they are

INDICATIONS

Straining compulsively and unremittingly towards a goal
Obsessive, meticulous, over-attention to detail
Critical of self and others
Impulsive or fixated in problem solving
Compensating strategies concealing feelings of inadequacy
Lack of satisfaction drives a need for self-gratification

AFFIRMATION: I see the very best in everyone and everything.

CROSS REFERENCE

Acceptance I Addictions I Attention I Creativity I Criticism I Frustration I Insecurity
Materialism I Negativity I Obsession I Obstinate I Optimism I Patience I Perfectionism
Sadness I Self-acceptance I Self-criticism I Self-sabotage I Thinking/Thought patterns
Tolerance I Will I Workaholic I Worry

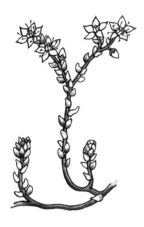

STONECROP
Sedum anglicum

TRANSITION

The language of flowers lists stonecrop's meaning as tranquillity. According to folklore, the essence of the stonecrop flower heals broken and wounded hearts. The one certainty in life is change. Change is never ceasing and is essential to growth. A caterpillar changes into a butterfly, abandons its attachments to its past, transforms its body into something new and more beautiful and emerges from darkness into light.

For many people, it is the fear of change that holds them back; fear of insecurity, of getting lost and being at the mercy of unknown forces. We resist change because we feel comfortable where we are. The cost of resistance is discontent, restlessness and frustration.

Stonecrop flower essence helps you to shift your consciousness to your centre, to the point of stillness and peace within. Even in the quietude you sense subtle, perpetual movement and accept that in times of transition you need to be patient and respect the process.

Real transformation takes place when you find your inner peace, accept you are in a period of transition and progress from there. You realise that you are not alone, that everything is in a constant state of growth and adaption and, like the butterfly, you will emerge from your cocoon, resplendent and free.

ATTRIBUTES

Stay calm while in process of personal transformation

Break through and break free of resistance

Accept what challenges you with calm composure

Embrace and welcome growth and expansion

Will and steady resolve to move forward into the new

Patience and forbearance while in the process of transition

INDICATIONS

Resistance to change and transition

Attachments and barriers that hold you back

Loneliness and isolation

Emotional holding on

Needing to break free from outworn routines and habits

Feeling restless and restricted

AFFIRMATION: I maintain my inner stillness and calm while welcoming change and transformation in my life.

CROSS REFERENCE

Acceptance I Alienation I Blocks I Birth and Birthing I Breakthrough I Calm I Change Death and Dying I Freedom I Frustration I Holding on Loneliness I Non-attachment Patience I Perseverance I Release I Resistance I Restlessness I Separation I Stagnation Transition I Transformation I Will

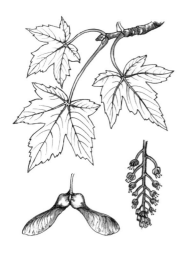

SYCAMORE
Acer pseudoplatanus

REVITALISATION

The sycamore is a species of the maple group known for its hardness and toughness and is attributed with the qualities of balance, practicality, peace and immortality. Sycamore symbolises the grounding force of the vital life energies that endow strength and staying power.

Psychic overload and nervous exhaustion from strain and over-striving can wear you down over time. Stress is often a precipitating factor, resulting in energy imbalances and a reduction in life energy, with accompanying negative emotional indications. A certain amount of stress is normal and can help get work done but when it is continuous, unremitting and unrelieved – persistently pushing yourself to the limit, for example – it is harmful to the body and mind.

The way we think determines our feelings and behaviour and how we respond or react to outer circumstances, whether with calm and ease or hurriedness and stress. Sycamore flower essence can help to relax unrealistic expectations you have of yourself and others. When you feel constrained, it helps to ease inner tension, thereby giving strength and perseverance with objectivity.

Standing your ground minimises the effect of the stresses of everyday life and increases the vitality of the basic life force. Welcome the stillness, solidity and clarity when you tap into and embrace your unlimited energy source, and experience the smooth flow of the energies in yourself and in your life.

- De-stress and restore the smooth flow of vital life energies
- Calm and gentle strength and perseverance
- Recognising the need to moderate your lifestyle to better manage inner tensions
- Freedom from inner driving impulses
- Continuity of effort through enhanced staying power
- Take time to allow your system to relax and recover

INDICATIONS

- Over-aroused, over-extended lifestyle giving rise to depletion
- Wearying inner disquiet
- Psychic overload and nervous exhaustion from strain and over-striving
- Deep discontent driving the impulse to achieve
- Weariness, anger and frustration when things don't go the way you want
- Frustrated ambition creates inner tension and tiredness

AFFIRMATION: I enjoy the smooth and gentle flow of energies in myself and in life.

CROSS REFERENCE

Ageing | Body | Energy | Fatigue | Flexibility | Frustration | Immunity | Lethargy | Life force
Lightness | Nervousness | Rejuvenation | Relaxation | Soothing | Strength | Stress
Tension | Tolerance | Vitality | Workaholic

THISTLE
Cirsium vulgare

COURAGE

Thistle is the national emblem of Scotland and an ancient Celtic symbol representing nobility of character. This mighty plant's wild spirit is a symbol of bravery, endurance and loyalty.

Acute stress, whether from internal or external circumstances, can trigger the body's 'fight or flight' response, a genetic wisdom designed to protect us from harm. When this automatic response is activated, the rational mind is disengaged and thinking becomes distorted. With the perceived threat of danger, the heart *chakra* closes down as fear arises. Real danger to physical survival aside, the fight or flight response is also triggered by our everyday modern world stresses, precipitating behavioural responses that can be self-defeating and work against your emotional, psychological and spiritual wellbeing.

Thistle flower essence can help to give you the courage to cope with a crisis. Courage is not the absence of fear but the power to triumph over fear. This essence helps to access inner strength and willpower, to remain calm and think clearly in any emergency, and to harness the willpower to respond with positive, intelligent action.

- Courage and conviction of action
- Willpower to overcome adversity
- Think clearly in an emergency
- Strength and force in the heart
- State of calm awareness and grounding
- Sense of inner security and strength

INDICATIONS

- Fear that brings you to a standstill
- Excessive over-reaction to perceived threats; panic
- Feeling powerless and vulnerable
- Over-reaction to events that are not life threatening
- Post-traumatic stress
- Invasive thoughts and fears inhibit performance

AFFIRMATION: I have the courage and strength to stand in my truth.
I bring confidence and certainty into all my actions.

CROSS REFERENCE

Action ǀ Anxiety ǀ Assertiveness ǀ Calm ǀ Confidence ǀ Courage ǀ Crisis ǀ Emergency
Empowerment ǀ Endurance ǀ Fear ǀ Grounding ǀ Insecurity ǀ Panic ǀ Power ǀ Protection
Shock ǀ Strength ǀ Stress ǀ Trauma ǀ Vulnerability ǀ Will

VALERIAN
Valeriana officinalis

DELIGHT

Valerian is known for its relaxing effect on body and mind. The World Health Organization recognises the use of valerian as a nerve relaxant. In the language of flowers it is attributed with 'an accommodating disposition'.

Some people find it hard to slow down and just be. In this fast-paced culture, it's easy to get caught up in entrenched habits and routines, where even leisure times can seem as if they are filled with endless activities. Being too ingrained in your habitual lifestyle, doing several activities at the same time, rushing and striving to get the next task completed, all create stress. Stress is inherent in living but you cannot allow stress to stand between you and the joys of life.

Valerian flower essence helps you to stay grounded and to focus your attention in the present. Being grounded means being fully present, physically, emotionally and mentally. One of the main benefits of living in the present moment is an improved ability to concentrate – your mind does not wander, you do not dwell on the past nor worry about the future.

Many of life's pleasures have to be enjoyed in the moment. There are opportunities to experience joy every day, if you open your heart to take a moment to find the joy in living. Be aware of the times when you get caught up in the buzz. Slow down, then stop and smell the flowers.

Stay focused, get more done and find more time so that you can live in the moment

Get your busy mind to slow down

Lighten up and have more fun

Enjoy life as it comes by being "in the now"

Tackle your problems with a sense of humour

Attain greater rhythm and balance in work and play

INDICATIONS

Tension in mind and body from hurry and worry

Not taking the time to really enjoy work or play

Being too ingrained in routines, with a general lack of joy

Self-torment, that if you don't keep on going you'll run out of steam

Restless, overactive and anxious mind disturbs sleeping patterns

Excessively worried about schedules and taking on too much

AFFIRMATION: I delight in the happiness of living
and I walk my spiritual path with lightness and humour.

CROSS REFERENCE

Awareness ı Centering ı Enthusiasm ı Fatigue ı Inner child ı Habit patterns ı Joy ı Lightness
Nervousness ı Openness ı Playfulness ı Patience ı Relaxation ı Restlessness ı Sleep
patterns ı Stress ı Tension ı Workaholic ı Worry

CLEAR STAGNANT ENERGIES AND
SOUND A VIBRATIONAL NOTE
OF PURITY. TRANSFORM YOUR
THOUGHTS AND EMOTIONS AND
REVEAL THE TRUE YOU.

WATERCRESS
Rorippa nasturtium aquaticum

WELLBEING

Watercress has been used for its medicinal properties for centuries. The Greeks and Romans thought it improved the brain. Stimulating and restorative, it is known to revitalise the body by cleansing the blood of impurities.

A cause of predisposition to illness can be karmic energetic patterns manifesting as chronic tendencies. Recent research suggests that these tendencies might derive their power through the memory of water. Unconscious psychological constructs and belief systems that become 'stuck' cause emotional and mental congestion that foments friction in the subtle bodies. For example, you can inherit or acquire fears, complexes and phobias that underpin your thoughts and attitudes and undermine emotional health and wellbeing. Inherent, dormant issues can then present themselves when your defences are down due to the derangement of the vital life force.

Watercress flower essence facilitates a cleansing process that aids the release of stagnant energies in the subtle bodies so that your energies are free to flow 'like a river'. As you come into harmony with your true self and homeostasis is restored, the emotions are calmed and you can find peace of mind.

Hidden aspects of the self, lost in the unconscious, can be retrieved and redeemed with self-awareness. Watercress' cleansing energy enables the mind to reflect its purity through the clarity of thought. This can manifest as spontaneous insights or the shining forth of the intuition guiding your expression and inspiration through right speech, creative intelligence and discrimination.

Cleanse and clear stagnant energies

Stimulate and strengthen inner defences

Cool down, remain calm, and stay collected

Take the edge off your emotional reactions

A clear and tranquil mind

Creating positive intentions

INDICATIONS

Being aware of energetic patterns of underlying chronic tendencies

Stagnant energies and deviation of the vital life force

Friction that leads to irritation in the subtle bodies

Strong moods put you on the defensive

Negative emotional reactions that present when your defences are down

Irritable, bad tempered

AFFIRMATION I cleanse my body and reflect the purity of my soul.

CROSS REFERENCE

Addiction | Anger | Body | Blocks | Calm | Catharsis | Clarity | Cleansing | Criticism
Defensiveness | Habit patterns | Immunity | Intolerance | Irritability | Materialism
Mood swing | Protection | Resistance | Stagnation | Temper | Thinking/Thought patterns
Transformation

WILD PANSY
Viola tricolor

RESONANCE

Wild pansy, also commonly known as 'heartsease', has a long history of use in herbal medicine. The flower represents memories, loving thoughts, togetherness and union. It is a plant of power that can heal the heart and illuminate the mind so that peace and clarity may prevail.

Fear blocks love and without love you cannot truly thrive. Fear disconnects you from the loving being that is your true nature. Love is the energy that fuels your life and if its flow is obstructed it is similar to the lifeblood flowing through the veins being obstructed. All manner of unsettling thoughts, sensations and emotions may then arise such as anxiety, fear, panic and disorientation.

Wild pansy's radiating energies bring love and warmth into the heart. Opening up and being receptive to the flow of life force or *prana* clears resistance to the energy of love rhythmically streaming forth, restoring body and mind harmony. Interconnection and flow of energy from the heart to the head is firmly established, so that the head *chakra* is vivified and becomes clear. This flower essence gives the sense of stability, and the feeling of safety from which you can open your heart, and feel your emotions.

ATTRIBUTES

Open to receive and radiate the energy of love

Strengthen sense of self and experience true connection

Flowing of life force and *prana* re-establishes rhythm and stability

Command of emotions and thoughts, especially when under stress

Presence of mind; composure

Clarity strengthening thought and mental processes

INDICATIONS

Not feeling connected to yourself due to the anxiety in your system

Loss of mental coherence and clarity, confusion

Anxiety can trigger dizziness and lack of concentration

Panic when you feel threatened; unable to manage your fear

Delay between thought and experience can create sensation of unreality

Dissipated or constricted energy flow between the heart and head centres

AFFIRMATION: My mind and my heart are open. I radiate light and love.

CROSS REFERENCE

Anxiety I Attention I Blocks I Calm I Clarity I Concentration I Confusion I Delusion I Energy
Fear I Insecurity I Life I Force I Nervousness I Openness I Panic I Receptivity I Resistance
Restlessness I Separation I Tension I Worry

WILLOWHERB
Chamaenerion angustifolium

SELF MASTERY

Willowherb is a prolific herb with medicinal benefits. It is a pioneer species as its seeds are first to colonise an area after a fire. In plant symbolism it is associated with pretentiousness. This plant exemplifies determination and tenacity. It has a passionate and fiery quality with a tendency to 'throw caution to the wind'. When faced with situations that upset your emotional and mental balance, you can speak out or act without due consideration or thought as to the costs or consequences, and the power of your emotions may be unhelpful or even harmful. Loss of control is a feature in episodes of imprudent emotional release. When you feel out of control and act out impulsively, you may live to regret your actions.

Negative emotional reactions to stressful events are natural and human and, to some degree, inevitable. Willowherb flower essence helps to calm your emotional body through awareness and conscious mindfulness. You may not be able to eliminate adverse emotional reactions but you can change your response to your emotions through knowing you have control of your feelings, much like you have control over other choices you make in your life.

True self-control can prevail through the right use of the will to regulate your emotions and behaviour in your aspiration for equanimity. By tempering the force of your personality with true power from your higher self, instead of reacting to your thoughts or feelings, your actions are governed by thoughtfulness, wisdom and goodwill. By taking the stance of the detached observer, you stay mindful and watchful and remain cool, calm and composed, even under provocation.

ATTRIBUTES

Adept use of will and power

Channel your fiery energies to good ends

Self-mastery of inner driving impulses

Cool, calm and composed even under provocation

Taking responsibility for, and owning, your emotional reactions

Balanced state of mind realised by the absence of strong attachments

INDICATIONS

Impulsive, irrepressible rush of emotion

Moods that restrict self-monitoring capacity and objectivity

Difficulty keeping powerful emotions in check

Easily provoked, excitable passions

Emotions controlling you rather than you controlling them

Negative impact of speech or action without thinking

AFFIRMATION: I master my personality and power. I bring humility and right use of will into all areas of my life.

CROSS REFERENCE

Anger | Awareness | Bullying | Calm | Catharsis | Control | Criticism | Hostility | Integration Intolerance | Irritability | Mood swing | Obstinate | Passion | Patience | Power | Temper | Will

WINTERGREEN
Moneses uniflora

GLADNESS

Wintergreen keeps its head bowed low and out of view until mature. It is reputed to be edible, high in vitamin C and in recent years was discovered to contain a new antibiotic. 'Dark night of the soul' is a metaphor used to describe a phase in a person's spiritual life marked by a sense of loneliness and despair. As darkness pervades the psyche, we become a witness to the shadow side of our personality. Seeing this shadow, we encounter powerlessness in the face of our deep suffering. In times of inner and outer darkness we can feel utterly alone, even when surrounded by others. It is the loneliness while surrounded by those who seek to understand and help which reinforces the darkness.

Yet, this experience of loneliness, of feeling bereft of support and protection, becomes an opportunity. Only in the stress of challenging circumstances can the full power of the soul be evoked. Wintergreen flower essence initiates the awakening or expansion of consciousness that invokes support from the soul. We call in our higher power to persevere, no matter how disinclined we are to do so, and no matter how extreme the inner turmoil. Pain opens the heart to love and understanding. Surrendering to receive love and guidance from the soul opens the heart to love and support from others.

Our search for meaning in the world is based on achieving a clear sense of personal identity. 'Dark night of the soul' therefore symbolises the dissolution of this sense of separate identity. From the unity of personal self and true self, meaning and purpose become clear. It is the reward for action and effort that leads you out of darkness and into the light.

Maintain your conscious connection no matter what

Remain mindful in the face of inevitable trial and tribulation

Open to receive love and attract support from others

Trust and follow your conscience and guidance

Stay positive with patient, optimistic expectancy

Uncomplaining acceptance, endurance and perseverance

INDICATIONS

Trauma leading to a period of great despair

The desolation of loneliness

Fear of collapse or breakdown

Feeling of standing alone against seemingly insurmountable odds

'Dark night of the soul'

Spiritual crisis or emergency

AFFIRMATION: I gladly embrace all the challenges life brings. I am positive in myself.

CROSS REFERENCE

Abandonment I Acceptance I Anxiety I Awareness I Courage I Crisis I Darkness I Death and Dying I Depression I Despair I Fear I Grief I Heartache I Higher self I Insecurity I Isolation Light I Loneliness I Optimism I Pain I Patience I Purpose I Release I Sadness I Self-pity Separation I Shadow self I Spiritual connection I Spiritual emergence I Strength I Stress Surrender I Tension I Trust

Combination
Essences

BABY BLUES

Supporting emotional change after birth

Sudden separation following the achievement of a cycle can cause upheaval and the sense of an emotional anticlimax. Baby Blues can help you to tap inner reserves of energy and strength to overcome weariness, uncertainty and anxiety and to be reassured and to stay calm.

Ancient Yew helps free up the feeling of being restricted or confined

Balsam tenderness, love and nurturing

Gorse renewal of life force, vitality, hope and joy

Holy Thorn open the heart to love and acceptance

Scottish Primrose relaxed and peaceful; staying power

Sea Rocket restore and replenish inner reserves of energy

Snowdrop inner strength and resilience; hope and optimism

Wintergreen uncomplaining acceptance, endurance and perseverance

BIRTHING

Open up naturally to conscious birthing

Anxiety, fear or self-limiting belief patterns can inhibit the spontaneous processes of giving birth. Birthing essence can help you to relax and let go with openhearted expectancy to the successful culmination of a new birth and a new beginning.

Balsam nurturing body and soul; relationship bonding

Cabbage power, motivation and strength to follow through

Grass of Parnassus openhearted; emotional receptivity and vulnerability

Hazel trust in the progression of events and 'go with the flow'

Lady's Mantle mind-body connection for optimal mental and physical performance

Scottish Primrose promotes feelings of relaxation and peacefulness

Stonecrop maintain balance through a transition

BON VOYAGE

To offset the negative effects of travel stress and fatigue

Travel can disturb natural rhythms. Bon Voyage can help you to find balance to cope with motion and calm to over-come fear, so that you to arrive feeling 'ready to go'.

Daisy calm, safe and focused

Sycamore recharge and uplift body and soul when stressed or fatigued

Scots Pine balance to cope with motion

Scottish Primrose relaxation and inner peace; restore natural rhythms

Wild Pansy circulation of energies following fluctuating or disturbed energy currents; disorientation

Sea Rocket refresh and rehydrate; adapt to change and flourish

CALM ME DOWN

Focus dynamic energy into intelligent creative activity

Foster calmness of mind and body through self-mastery of negative emotions that impede clear thinking, concentration and composure. Calm Me Down helps to integrate the mental and emotional bodies, which aids your ability to pay attention and channel energies into right action.

Bell Heather self confidence; centred individuality

Daisy stay calm; feel safe

Lady's Mantle bring the light of consciousness into the unconscious

Laurel bring about order and organisation

Monkey Flower self-assurance; courage to overcome problems

Wild Pansy presence of mind and composure

Willowherb self-control; self-mastery over inner driving impulses

CLEAR LIGHT

For bringing about a peaceful state of mind

By stilling and focusing the mind, Clear Light can influence mental clarity and brightness and assist in attuning to higher wisdom and inspiration. An excellent aid for meditation and study.

concentration and clarity

open-minded and clear perception

integrating rational thinking and the intuitive mind

practical and creative expression of intuition

trust your inner knowing and intuition

presence of mind and composure

ENERGY SHIELD

ENERGY SHIELD

To cleanse and protect the energy field

Energy Shield helps you to stand in strength and create the positive energy that you need to feel more confident to handle detrimental vibrations that affect you. Energy Shield helps to purify, transform and release negative energies and influences.

Scottish Primrose fosters a sense of inner peace and calm

Watercress clear stagnant energies and strengthen inner defences

Wild Pansy enhance receptivity to and increase circulation of life force

Wintergreen stand in strength during crisis or emergency

Hematite purify negative energies; clear and calm the mental body

Diamond foster fearlessness and a sense of invincibility

Element essences of Earth, Water, Fire, Air and Ether stabilise the etheric *chakra* system by the regular anchoring of the life force

EROS

Nurture love, sensitivity and intimacy

Without self-acceptance it is difficult to love and nurture yourself or be a loving partner. Eros can help you to relax, enjoy and be in tune with your body.

Balsam open to intimacy; love and nurture the physical and emotional body

Elder reveal and radiate your inner beauty and vitality

Gorse enthusiasm, passion and enjoyment

Grass of Parnassus openness, tenderness and sensitivity

Rose Alba effective creative self-expression; patience; staying power

Sea Pink balance and harmonise your inner dualities

Sycamore draw on inner reserves of strength, softness and flexibility

Holy Thorn loving acceptance; open your heart to love

FEMININITY

Support for women's issues and cycles

During times of changing rhythms or mood swings, Femininity can help you to release tension and restore emotional balance and wellbeing.

Balsam love and nurture the physical body; emotional availability

Holy Thorn self-love and acceptance

Elder vibrancy and vitality; stimulate recuperative powers of the body

Sea Rocket foster an inner sense of security and stability; refresh and replenish

Scottish Primrose relaxation, inner harmony and peace

Sycamore restore softness and gentleness to your energy flow

Rowan release tension and pain

Lady's Mantle balance and harmonise your mood and temperament

FERTILITY

Co-Creation of a new heart and soul

Stress and emotional imbalance can impede the processes of naturally conceiving. Fertility can help open your heart to love, to being impregnated with a new way of being and creativity, and to the emergence of a fresh impetus in life.

Ancient Yew spontaneous action that leads to new directions for growth

Balsam love and nurture the physical and emotional body

Grass of Parnassus openness; letting down barriers

Holy Thorn open the heart to love and intimacy

Hawthorn acceptance; tender-heartedness

Elf Cup Lichen clear deep-seated patterns and emotions

Sea Rocket building a sense of self that is resilient and strong

FIRST AID

Calming, soothing relief in any crisis

In times of stress or trauma, First Aid can help to relieve associated fear and anxiety, and ease pain and tension.

Daisy feel calm, safe and centred

Scottish Primrose relaxed and peaceful

Bell Heather inner strength, resilience and self-confidence

Thistle courage to take positive action

GO WITH THE FLOW
Enjoy the freedom of movement

When limitations that restrict ease of movement hold you back, Go With The Flow can help you to release tension and relax. When your energies flow smoothly, so do you, and with graceful, effortless movement.

Cabbage motivation; mobilise your will and intention

Globethistle strength, flexibility and endurance

Hazel perseverance; difficult things seem easy

Holy Thorn self-acceptance without limitation

Ragged Robin release blocks and allow life force energies to flow

Rowan release tension and pain

Stonecrop be patient with yourself; break through and break free

Sycamore smooth and effortless energy flow

Watercress catalyst to purify and clear stagnant energies

Willowherb self-mastery; stay cool and calm

HEALING THE CAUSE
Strength and support to get well

Deep-seated or long-standing negative emotions hinder the ability to get well. Healing the Cause can help you to take charge of your own health, surrender obstacles to wholeness and wellbeing, and heal the past and sources of suffering.

Ancient Yew release burdens and clear obstacles

Gorse vitality, hope and joy

Elf Cup Lichen clear and cleanse deep-seated emotional trauma

Monkey Flower courage to face and transcend your fears

Rowan release resentment and pain; forgive and heal the past

Snowdrop optimism and hope

Sycamore strength, flexibility and endurance

Watercress release and purify stagnant energies, and strengthen your inner defences

HEART SUPPORT

**To heal the heart when affected
by trauma or grief**

For all issues connected with the heart
and love, Heart Support can help you
to feel supported during major life
changes that cause stress and tension.

Scottish Primrose peace of mind,
serenity and calm

Stonecrop patience, inner stillness
and quietude

Rowan release tension and pain;
heal the past

Grass of Parnassus open the heart
to the healing power of love

Holy Thorn love, acceptance and
compassion

Wild Pansy clear mind and open heart;
clear and balance distorted energy
patterns

Gorse uplift the heart and mind

Rose Water Lily strength and
courage of heart

HOLY GRAIL

**To integrate and harmonise
the physical, emotional, mental
and spiritual bodies**

Holy Grail can help bring balance and
harmony into all aspects of your life
through alignment and synthesis of
body, mind and soul. Embody and express your full creative potential.

Balsam bountiful embodiment
of vitality

Lady's Mantle integrating the rational
and intuitive mind

Rose Alba positive outgoing creativity;
intuitive power expressed in words
and action

Globethistle wholeness through
synthesising personality power
and soul force

INNER CHILD

Nurturing Your Inner Child

When you react from childhood emotional wounds and attitudes, your experiences of the past dictate how you respond to life today. Inner Child may help to change your behaviour patterns and to honour the child you were, in order to love the person you are.

Daisy playfulness; emotional calm and composure

Grass of Parnassus heal and transform the past

Gorse enjoyment and celebration of life

Harebell live in the awareness that all is well in your world

Lady's Mantle enlightened emotional balance and harmony

Sea Holly let down your self-protective barriers; calm confidence

Wintergreen open to receive love and attract support from others

KARMA CLEAR

To release the tensions that bring pain, suffering and unhappiness

Karma Clear can help you heal the past through compassion and forgiveness and by awareness and understanding of the underlying causes of life's predicaments and ailments.

Birch insight through broadening your perception and understanding

Snowdrop optimism; transformation through surrender and detachment

Rowan release resentment and pain; forgive and heal the past

Holy Thorn open the heart to love and acceptance

Cherry transcend inherited karmic predispositions

Elf Cup Lichen clear and cleanse deep-seated emotional trauma

LIFE FORCE

To overcome tiredness, low energy or burnout

Life Force can help to uplift body and soul when you feel weary or drained of energy. Activate the vital life force and stimulate the body's powers of renewal.

Gorse vitality, dynamism and enthusiasm

Elder stimulate the body's natural powers of rejuvenation

Sycamore calm and gentle strength, and perseverance

Valerian lighten up and be lively

Grass of Parnassus give of yourself, openly and wholeheartedly

LIGHT BEING

Be content and enjoy life

Light Being can help to uplift your spirits when feelings of despair, sadness or hopelessness weigh down on your soul. Identifying with a greater sense of purpose and nurturing an optimistic outlook on life, contentment and happiness can be achieved in the present moment.

Gorse light-heartedness and joy

Holy Thorn open the heart to self love, acceptance and compassion

Rose Water Lily courage of heart and peace of mind

Snowdrop optimism and hope; serenity and peace through acceptance

Spotted Orchid have a more positive outlook

Valerian cheerful and light-hearted

Wintergreen patience, endurance and perseverance

MASCULINITY

Discovering the secret of the masculine soul

Masculinity may help when you get caught up in cultural and traditional 'masculine' roles and expectation, to get in touch with and free your feeling nature. The willingness to move from power to love reveals a soul strong enough to accept vulnerability and to be authentic.

Cabbage power and strength to achieve your goals

Globethistle inner strength to free yourself from a sense of 'duty'

Grass of Parnassus openness, gentleness and sensitivity

Holy Thorn open the heart to acceptance, compassion and self-love

Lime realisation of inner reconciliation of self with the whole

Rose Alba effective and creative self-expression

Sea Holly fearless in expressing and revealing yourself

PROSPERITY

Manifesting an abundance of wellbeing

Prosperity can help foster a sense of inner security and faith in yourself, and to align with the source of universal, limitless supply to manifest your dreams and goals.

Bell Heather faith, trust and confidence

Harebell self-reliant and secure in yourself

Elder stimulate powers of dynamism and enthusiasm

Laurel get organised to help bring your ideas into action

Sea Rocket adapt to change, succeed and flourish

Cabbage motivation and power to achieve your goals

Rose Alba creative power guided by the intuition

PSYCHIC PROTECTION

Protecting the emotional body against negative forces

Feel calm and centred by creating a safe space within you and, around you. Psychic Protection can help in detaching from negative thought forms or energies when you feel vulnerable, or in overwhelming situations or environments.

Daisy calm, centred and self-assured

Thistle sense of inner security and strength

Rose Alba connect with and direct your creative power

Watercress transform negative energies and strengthen your inner defences

Iona Pennywort clear judgement and discernment

Ancient Yew set clear boundaries and stand in your power

Wintergreen stay awake and aware, even in difficult times

SEASONAL AFFECTIONS

Sunshine in the soul when feeling under the weather

Seasonal Affections can help you to release emotional congestion, discomfort and irritation. Feel protected and supported, no matter what the season or prevailing conditions.

Birch clear vision; detach emotionally from worry or distress

Elder stimulate the body's natural powers of recuperation

Globethistle greater reserves of patience and flexibility

Gorse strengthen the life force and vitality

Scots Pine listen and pay attention to your body's needs

Snowdrop optimism and hope

Sycamore calm and gentle strength and endurance

Watercress purify causes of irritation and irritability

SEXUAL INTEGRITY

Awaken to loving intimacy

Sexual Integrity can help you to break old patterns and learn how to channel sexual energy in ways that nurture the body as well as the soul.

Balsam love and nurture the physical body; express warmth and tenderness

Daisy rediscovery of innocence; feel safe, calm and composed

Globethistle patience and flexibility

Holy Thorn open the heart to self-love and acceptance

Elf Cup Lichen release unconscious or deep-seated emotions

Rowan reconcile and heal the past

Scottish Primrose inner peace; open the heart to unconditional love

SPIRITUAL MARRIAGE

Integrate and harmonise the masculine and feminine qualities

Spiritual Marriage can help balance your inner pairs of opposites. Dynamic union of intuition and consciousness with intelligence and activity can free your full potential and maximise richness in the joy of right relationship.

Apple cultivate an open attitude and willing body and mind

Holy Thorn open your heart and reveal your true self

Mallow right relationship through harmonisation of head and heart, mind and feeling

Sea Pink balance and harmonise the energy flow between opposites

Elecampane open and receptive; connection and communication

SWEET DREAMS
Good night, sleep well

Sweet Dreams can help calm your energies and restore natural rhythms, with the result that you find balance and peace of mind.

Scottish Primrose relaxation; inner peace and harmony

Valerian lighten up when weighed down from hurry, worry, stress or tension

Lady's Mantle relax into deeper levels of consciousness; also helpful in understanding dreams and symbols

Grass of Parnassus soothing; gentleness and sensitivity

Birch release worries and cares and find peace of mind

TEENS
Spontaneity, focus and balance

Teens can help overcome the limitations that greater self-consciousness creates and help foster self-acceptance, understanding and confidence.

Birch open-minded; release your worries

Holy Thorn self-love and acceptance; openly express your feelings

Lady's Mantle balance and harmony of emotions and thoughts

Mallow clear and heartfelt communication

Rose Alba effective and creative self-expression

Sea Holly allow your inner light and beauty to shine

Sea Rocket foster an inner sense of stability, self-assurance and resilience

Spotted Orchid behold the beauty and perfection of the self

TRANSFORMATION

**Supporting personal growth
and transformation**

Transformation can help to harmonise seemingly opposing parts of you, cultivate your inner strength to persevere and stay on course, and help you to willingly make sacrifices that serve your highest good.

Apple clarity of purpose and intention

Grass of Parnassus heal and transform the past

Globe Thistle strength and willingness to make sacrifices

Sea Pink owning our disavowed parts and integrating the inner polarities

Watercress purify and clear stagnant energies

Iona Pennywort clear judgement and discernment; mastery over desires

Stonecrop willingness and patience to change

VOICE CONFIDENCE

**Express and radiate inner beauty
and confidence**

Voice Confidence can help you to free your expression and let creativity flow. With trust, and the motivation to succeed, your performance reflects calmness, composure and self-confidence.

Elecampane believe in yourself and your abilities

Garden Pea clear articulation and communication

Holy Thorn self-love and acceptance

Lady's Mantle mindful, balanced and conscious expression

Rose Alba channel creative power through words and action

Scots Pine listen and trust your own inner knowing and wisdom

Sea Holly let your light and beauty shine

Thistle inner security and strength; courage of heart

Sacred Space

TO BRING FORTH LIGHT, CLARITY AND SERENITY.

"Sacred Space" was created when we were asked which essences would be beneficial to cleanse and purify the Sanctuary (the Findhorn Foundation's original meditation space). We experimented with the elemental essences, which were combined and used in a spray mist.

As the elemental essences help to restore the health of the elements in the body, and strengthen the receptivity of life force or *prana* in the related *chakra*, it became evident that they could achieve a similar effect in a space. 'Sanctuary" spray was born and proved to be very effective. It centres, grounds and empowers with the invigorating vital life force of the elements.

The elemental essences of nature combine in Sacred Space to purify the atmosphere. Earth element represents foundations, stability, the physical realm and the power and beauty of the Earth. Water element is life giving, cleanses and purifies, and will flow into any space that allows it entry. It influences our subconscious forces. Fire element projects vitality and enthusiasm, and promotes creativity through its stirring radiant currents. Air element corresponds to the realm of the intellect and is also about communication. It is stimulating and brings inspiration, allowing your imagination to flow. Sacred Space also contains pure essential oils of Rose alba, the pure white rose, and Frankincense, that release a fine, delicate fragrance to further enhance the harmonious energy.

Sacred Space purifies and clears stressful or 'stuck' energy in the home, workplace and personal aura. It can be used professionally, for example in the busy work place, where negative energy emitted from computers, office equipment and stressed-out colleagues can seriously affect decision-making and your own stress levels. Sacred Space helps transmute negative energy, restores calm and tranquillity, and creates a more positive atmosphere in which to work, meditate, or simply "be".

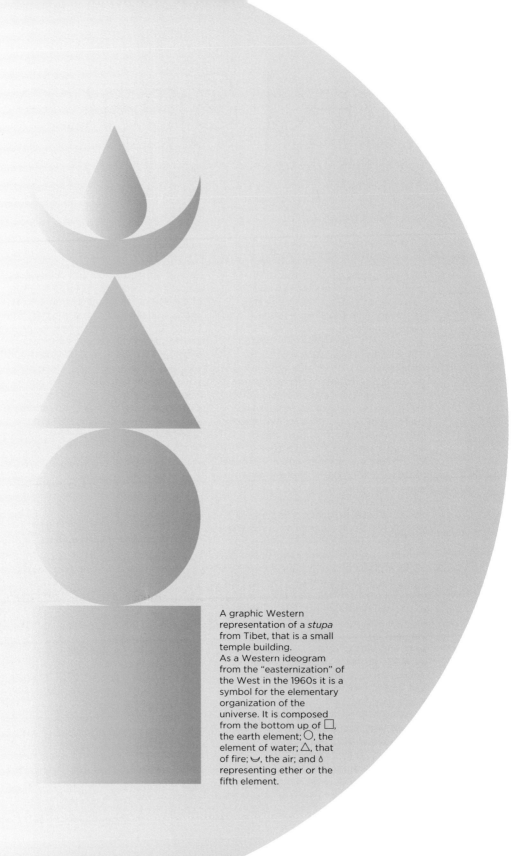

A graphic Western representation of a *stupa* from Tibet, that is a small temple building.
As a Western ideogram from the "easternization" of the West in the 1960s it is a symbol for the elementary organization of the universe. It is composed from the bottom up of □, the earth element; ○, the element of water; △, that of fire; ◡, the air; and ◊ representing ether or the fifth element.

Elemental Essences

THE FOUR ELEMENTS OF NATURE ARE CALLED INTO PLAY: "THE EARTH TO NURTURE THE PLANT, THE AIR FROM WHICH IT FEEDS, THE SUN OR FIRE TO ENABLE IT TO IMPART ITS POWERS AND WATER...TO BE ENRICHED WITH ITS BENEFICIENT MAGNETIC HEALING".

DR. EDWARD BACH

Flower essences are sometimes described as being alchemical. The great mystic healer and alchemist Paracelsus (1493-1541) used to collect the dew from plants with which to treat his patients. The alchemists regarded dew as a mystical medium, the vehicle of celestial influences, charged with the life force of the plants from which it is collected.

The four elements were first referred to in 450 BCE by the Greek philosopher Empedocles. His doctrine that the elements manifest in the body as spiritual essences and act in affinity with universal energies provided the foundation for understanding the elements. Aristotle's exposition of the theory of the elements held sway from 350 BCE until the emergence of the new generation of science in 17th century Europe.

The elements were held in such high esteem because they carried out the work of nature by combining and recombining to create all the different types of matter on earth. The elements were seen as forces or agencies found at the very heart of matter, rather than detectable substances.

The four basic elements of nature are earth, water, fire and air. Within each are elemental beings that are the spiritual essences of the element. The fifth element of ether unites them all within space.

According to the ancient Vedas, the *chakras* are tools of the elements and each of the five *chakras* along the spine is associated with a specific element that creates the internal environment, which changes in accordance with the energy of the element being radiated. The elements build up the forms of the subtle and physical bodies. They exist on all levels (or planes) and empower the functioning of the bodies. Any disease produces a distortion or impairs the elements in the body. If one of them is weak, the devitalised element will produce a dysfunction in the body in the location that is the sphere of its influence.

ELEMENTAL ESSENCES
The elemental essences work essentially to restore the health of the elements in the body and to strengthen the receptivity of life energies, or *prana,* in the related *chakra* or centre.

EARTH

Earth elemental essence works at the level of the 1st or base *chakra* and embodies the will to be oneself. It represents stability, security, balance and the ability to stand in strength in your power.
The earth element and therefore the essence strengthens the receptivity of life force in the base centre through concentration, patience, perseverance and discipline and leads to calm, dependable grounding of ideas, practicality and material abundance.

WATER

Water elemental essence works at the level of the 2nd or sacral *chakra* and nurtures love of family, friends and one's group. It fosters empathy, sensitivity and tenderness and the power to create harmonious emotional relationships.
The water element and therefore the essence strengthens the receptivity of life force in the sacral centre through receptivity, understanding, adaptability and imagination and assists in relaxing and maintaining a peaceful and magnetic personality.

FIRE

Fire elemental essence works at the level of the 3rd or solar plexus *chakra* and stimulates aspiration towards the ideals of the soul through self-confidence, enthusiasm, optimism, passion and the desire to help others.

The fire element and therefore the essence strengthens the receptivity of life force in the solar plexus centre through cognition and alertness of mind that brings self-reliance, courage and leadership skills, increasing vitality in all areas of life and the ability to take forthright action.

AIR

Air elemental essence works at the level of the 4th or heart *chakra,* as well as the 5th or throat *chakra* and upholds the intuition, and the expression of unconditional love, sympathy, emotional independence and personal refinement.

The air element and therefore the essence strengthens the receptivity of life force in the heart centre through perceptiveness and objectivity, leads to clear comprehension and discernment and helps in developing dexterity and enterprise skills in intuiting practical solutions.

ETHER

Ether elemental essence works at the level of the 5th or throat *chakra,* as well as the 6th or *ajna chakra* and 7th or crown *chakra,* and exists as quintessential life force. It concerns the expression of the consciousness.

The ether element and therefore the essence strengthens the receptivity of life force in the throat centre, develops the instinctual intuition, mental flexibility, creative intelligence and right speech and manifests as spiritual love and the power of synthesis. Ether element essence is the 'quintessence', the fifth element, the mother and creator of the four elements. All the other elements arise from the fifth or spiritual etheric realm.

Exaltation and Wesak Blessing Essences

THE ESOTERIC BACKGROUND TO EXALTATION AND WESAK BLESSING ESSENCES ARE DRAWN FROM THE AGELESS WISDOM TEACHINGS FROM THE WRITINGS OF A.A. BAILEY AND H.P. BLAVATSKY. THEY ARE GROUP ESSENCES.

EXALTATION ESSENCE

Exaltation was made at one Gemini full moon meditation in Universal Hall, Findhorn. We had been asked to bring a flower to the meditation, which was led by Eileen Caddy. As we gave our flower offering, we sent out a prayer and spoke a blessing into the world.

Flowers of gorse, broom, red poppy, yellow poppy, clover, red campion, white campion, rowan, rose, wild carrot, catmint, chives, wild ox-eyed daisy, japanese quince, honesty, brassica, lady's mantle, aquilegia, wild borage, vetch, wallflower, viper's bugloss, wild pansy, bluebell, grasses and the 'ten thousand things' of blessings were so beautiful, floating in the large, pentagonal-shaped copper bowl. This essence was of its own creation.

The energies that can be distributed at the Gemini festival are the special energies received at Wesak. Wisdom is expressed through light and love.

Exaltation essence works at the level of the 6th *ajna* or brow *chakra*. Soul or universal love energies work through the 'third eye', through the *ajna,* and coordinates all the other centres in unison to bring forth the spiritual will.

It blends the energies of *ajna,* heart and crown *chakras* and manifests as the spirit of goodwill expressed through the heart and mind.

Spiritual insight gained through the intuition, pure reason and comprehension of ideas can then be expressed through the formulation of ideals. When illumined by purity of motive and loving purpose, the energies of love and wisdom work out in true spiritual activity on the physical plane.

WESAK BLESSING

Legend has it that at the time of the full moon in May, when the sun is in the sign of Taurus, there is a very special gathering and ceremony held in the Wesak Valley in the Himalayas during which Buddha returns each year to pour blessings upon earth and humanity. In this ceremony, when the Buddha appears, a crystal bowl of water is blessed and the water distributed.

Wesak Blessing essence works at the level of the 7th or crown *chakra* and brings consciousness from the subtle and higher planes into definite working aware-ness. This is achieved by opening to divine inspiration and receiving those higher spiritual qualities of clear-sightedness, understanding and enlightenment into the crown *chakra* and distributing them through the *ajna.*

Intention is the invocation, by opening to the processes of spiritual perception through the intuition and by the clear pure light of divine understanding.

	EARTH	WATER	FIRE
PHYSICAL/ETHERIC	• builds up bones, muscles, tendons, organs, hair and nails • stability, security, balance and the ability to move forward • practicality and material abundance • the will to be; the will to live	• creation of forms (e.g. cells, an embryo) • builds up all the fluids (blood, lymph etc.) • relaxes and refreshes	• digestion and absorption to fuel the body • responsible for the body's temperature, inner combustion (e.g. stomach, intestines), enhances blood circulation • increases vitality in all areas of life, and helps in taking action
EMOTIONAL	• the will to either hold or let go • calm and dependable • mastery of negative emotions • develops the subtle sense of smell	• desire to create and protect that which is created • produces empathy, sensitivity and tenderness • maintains a peaceful and magnetic personality • creates harmonious emotional relationships • dissolves repressed emotions	• desire for pleasure and sweetness of life, aspiration • self-confidence, enthusiasm, optimism, passion and • the desire to help others • affects astral clairvoyance e.g. perception of auras
MENTAL	• the will to think • strengthens patience, perseverance, concentration and discipline • develops extreme sensitivity of touch and physical feeling	• self-education and a sense of responsibility • knowing, understanding, receptivity, adaptability and imagination • develops sensitivity to others' thoughts	• how one thinks about oneself • produces cognition, memory and alertness of mind • self-reliance, courage and leadership • develops mental clairvoyance e.g. perception of etheric body and its energetic functioning
SOUL	• the will to be oneself	• love of family, friends, one's group	• helps you to aspire to the ideals of the soul

AIR	ETHER	EXALTATION	WESAK
• circulation and immune discrimination response • produces gases: (e.g. gas exchange in the lungs) • developing dexterity, solutions to practical problems (e.g. enterprise skills)	• exists as pure life force • concerns the consciousness in the cells • inspires right speech	• direction and coordination of the endocrine system as a whole and linking with the brain	• regulates body rhythms and response to light
• unconditional love • sympathy, subtlety, emotional independence and refinement e.g. poise, gracefulness • developing clairaudience e.g. ability to hear the communications of the spirits in nature	• fosters a desire to serve others • manifests as love • develops the expression of the consciousness, the instinctual intuition	• engenders the love of the humanity and group love	• responsiveness and awareness of emotions
• justice and discrimination • creative intelligence • good analytical skills • clear comprehension • mental versatility • develops clairaudience and to access higher knowledge, the superconscious (universal) mind e.g. the ability to hear the music of the spheres	• encourages mental flexibility • manifests as the power of synthesis • develops the first forms of psychic abilities, inner communication or 'channelling'	• encourages spiritual study and understanding	• direction of thought
• intuition	• thinking as the soul • manifests as spiritual love • develops direct transmission, the higher psychic faculty	• observe and respond to soul direction	• seeing the vision in the light of the soul

Gem Essences of the Seven Rays

"FOR THE SOUL'S FORCES TO BE PROPERLY GROUNDED IN THE PHYSICAL PLANE THERE MUST BE A POINT OF FOCUS. CRYSTALS ARE THIS POINT OF FOCUS, BEING IN A CONSTANT STATE OF RESONANCY".

GEM ELIXIRS AND VIBRATIONAL HEALING VOL. 1, GURUDAS

Crystals and gemstones have been used since ancient times as medicines. There is a lot of literature, including ancient sources and sacred texts from around the world that recognise gemstones emit powerful energies.

THEIR MEDICAL AND MAGICAL PROPERTIES

The tradition of Ayurvedic medicine, for example, gives information as to their medical and magical properties. I think they are best understood in terms of their qualities.

When I was researching this literature, after having made the seven gem essences in 2003, I discovered C. Nelson Stewart's book *Gemstones of the Seven Rays*. In his book he quotes 'an enthusiastic worker among precious stones': "The brilliancy, the colour and the symmetrical crystal forms of precious stones have in all ages suggested to man some kind of indwelling life and the idea that precious stones are flowers that grow underground".

He states that gemstones, from their mineral geometric structure of "static equilibrium", confer "a state of acquiescence in the presence of molecular forces".

I have made the gem essences using the same sun infusion method I use to make flower essences. They are different from flower essences as their 'goal' is to be effective in clearing the *nadi*, the 'tubes or ducts' that are the foundation of the subtle etheric body, removing negativity that can impede the flow of life force to the *chakras*. Gem essences are traditionally used to treat *chakra* imbalances.

Gems and crystals have a natural alignment with electromagnetic fields and can be seen as reservoirs of pure radiating energy.

Their concentrated rays influence cellular activity at an atomic level, similar to the effect of infra-red rays, for example, whose low frequency rays create the feeling of heat by elevating ones atomic vibrational rate and moderating the endocrine system.

Gem essences help in grounding new qualities and energies in the person taking them by creating order and stability. They can facilitate or augment the healing power of flower essences. Information on the influence of the Seven Ray energies in the making of the gem essences comes from the literature in terms of the astrological timing for solarising the essence, the gemstones associated with the rays, and the literature on the qualities of the rays themselves.

The seven rays are streams of energy emanating from cosmic sources and are distributed to our solar system through constellations and planets. These rays are the origin of all existence in the solar system, including the human body. The primary ray of our solar system is the second ray of love and wisdom and the other six rays are in fact sub-rays of this second ray. Love is the primary quality being developed in our scheme. Each ray expresses a particular kind of force or energy. Rays constitute the fundamental energies of all forms with the emphasis on the distinctive quality – the vibration, colour and note that force exhibits – rather than the manifested form aspect it creates. Through its distinctive energy, a ray determines the quality of the astral/emotional nature, governs the mind, endows physical characteristics and conditions the distribution of energy through the etheric body and *chakra* system. The ray predisposes a person to certain strengths and weaknesses.

The soul ray manifests as the subtle energies of the higher or 'true' self that guides and influences the person from within through its bodies of expression – a physical/etheric body, an emotional body and a mental body. Each of these 'vehicles' is governed by one or other of the rays. The combining of the different rays is what distinguishes us and is why we are all different.

DIAMOND
ENERGY INFLUENCES OF RAY ONE
Astrological signs: *Aries, Leo, Capricorn*

SPIRITUAL ALIGNMENT
The essence of diamond focuses the first ray energies of will and power. Its purpose may assist to align to the vision and purpose of your higher self, and to attain through concentration of will. With a clear vision of the purpose you can prioritise, set objectives and focus on essentials.

Expansion of the capacity to love develops the virtues of tenderness, compassion, tolerance and fearlessness.

SOUL
Virtues of the Ray
- dynamic power
- strength in purpose
- courage
- steadfastness
- independence
- truthfulness

Virtues to be acquired
- love
- tenderness
- sympathy
- compassion
- patience
- tolerance
- humility

MIND
- clear vision of your purpose
- power to take responsibility
- setting objectives
- illumination and thought amplification
- cleansing effect on the mind
- fearlessness, invincibility
- detach from causes of irritation and fatigue

BODY
- crown *chakra*
- pineal gland
- cerebrum
- physical/etheric organs, systems and structures governed by the *chakra*
- problems and imbalances related to the head, upper brain and eye

POWER TO INTEGRATE WEAKNESSES OF
- excessive pride
- arrogance
- wilfulness
- destructiveness
- impatience, control and suppression
- feelings of isolation or being separate from others

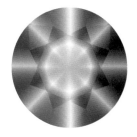

SAPPHIRE
ENERGY INFLUENCES OF RAY TWO
Astrological Signs: *Gemini, Virgo, Pisces*

CLARITY AND INTUITION
Essence of sapphire focuses the second ray energies of love and wisdom. These energies can help you to be calm and clear, and find peace of mind. Purity of thought and an expanded understanding and awareness will lead to illumination, insight and intuition. Compassion for, and selfless service to others, evokes the power to heal, teach and inspire through love.

SOUL

Virtues of the Ray

- radiance
- magnetism
- wisdom
- sensitivity to the whole/ inclusiveness
- spiritual power
- intuition
- power to heal through love

Virtues to be acquired

- fearlessness
- love
- compassion
- selflessness
- tangible service

MIND

- serenity
- joy
- peace
- faith
- equanimity
- strengthened compassion and the sense of community
- expanded understanding and awareness
- love for truth
- purity of mind, mental clarity and perception, astuteness

BODY

- heart *chakra*
- thymus gland
- mid-brain
- physical/etheric organs, systems and structures governed by the *chakra*
- problems and imbalances related to the heart, blood, circulatory system, vagus nerve

POWER TO INTEGRATE WEAKNESSES OF

- fear
- self-pity
- oversensitivity
- insecurity
- attachment
- coldness and indifference
- indecision

EMERALD
ENERGY INFLUENCES OF RAY THREE
Astrological Signs: *Cancer, Libra, Capricorn*

BALANCE AND COMMUNICATION
The essence of emerald focuses the third ray energies of active, creative intelligence. These energies facilitate accessing the intelligent and intuitive mind that aids you in manifesting your plan. With devotion to concentration, you may attain right understanding and enhanced communication skills. Realise the will to succeed by tolerance, accuracy, creative adaptability and practical, planned activity.

SOUL

Virtues of the Ray
- sincerity of purpose
- wide views on all abstract questions
- clear intellect
- intuition
- capacity for concentration
- adaptability

Virtues to be acquired
- tolerance
- devotion
- accuracy
- commonsense

MIND
- mental illumination
- clear intellect and thinking
- enhanced memory, communication and speech
- seeking and realising objectives, practical efficiency, success in business

BODY
- throat *chakra* (also sacral *chakra*)
- thyroid
- medulla
- physical/etheric organs, systems and structures governed by the *chakra*
- problems and imbalances related to the lungs, bronchial and vocal parts, alimentary canal, reproductive organs (sacral *chakra*)

POWER TO INTEGRATE WEAKNESSES OF
- hyperactivity
- impulsiveness
- verbosity
- insensitivity
- opportunism, selfish manipulation
- vagueness
- confusion
- intellectualism
- criticism, irritation and frustration

JASPER
ENERGY INFLUENCES OF RAY FOUR
Astrological Signs: *Taurus, Scorpio, Sagittarius*

IMAGINATION AND CREATIVITY

Essence of jasper focuses the fourth ray energies of harmony through conflict. Realise beauty and harmony by unifying opposing forces. Cultivate stamina for ongoing projects through mental and emotional balance and serenity. By inner harmony and unity, the will to harmonise and make peace is evoked and the confidence to express yourself creatively through the power of beauty.

SOUL

Virtues of the Ray

- love of beauty
- love of colour
- creative living
- strong affections and passions
- high intuition
- sense of drama
- musicality
- artistic impulse
- the ability to make peace

Virtues to be acquired

- mental and emotional balance
- serenity, confidence
- self-control
- purity
- selflessness
- accuracy
- power to express divinity

MIND

- courage to speak out and have personal independence
- creativity, harmony
- clear vision, dissolves illusion
- calm mind and emotions, relief from stress
- eases the resolving of conflicts, avoid extremes
- ability to grow through struggle and crisis
- strong affections, fighting spirit

BODY

- base centre (and also *ajna*/brow *chakra*)
- adrenals
- cerebellum
- physical/etheric organs, systems and structures governed by the *chakra*
- problems and imbalances of the skeletal system, especially the spine, kidney system, endocrine system (*ajna chakra*)

POWER TO INTEGRATE WEAKNESSES OF

- anxiety, worry and agitation
- excessive moodiness
- unregulated passions
- self-absorption
- procrastination
- addiction to drama
- impulsiveness
- instability
- exaggeration

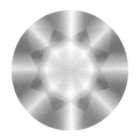

TOPAZ
ENERGY INFLUENCES OF RAY FIVE
Astrological signs: *Leo, Sagittarius, Aquarius*

LUCIDITY AND INVENTIVENESS

The essence of topaz focuses the fifth ray energies of concrete knowledge and science.

Access the higher mind and think with clarity. Invoke the will to patience, persistence and wide mindedness and keep all aspects of yourself in balance. Through concentration, observation and practical inventiveness, achieve mastery in a field of knowledge, and the power to realise great plans.

SOUL

Virtues of the Ray
- focused intellect
- accuracy and precision
- perseverance
- common sense
- practical inventiveness
- the power to create thought forms

Virtues to be acquired
- love
- sympathy
- reverence
- devotion
- broadmindedness

MIND
- power to initiate activity, to realise great plans
- power to discriminate, inventiveness, precision, logical analysis
- self-confidence
- truthfulness
- supports the ability to stand back and observe the self

BODY
- *ajna chakra* (also throat and sacral *chakras*)
- pituitary
- peripheral nerves
- physical/etheric organs, systems and structures governed by the *chakra* problems and imbalances related to lower brain, eyes, ears, nose, endocrine and nervous systems

POWER TO INTEGRATE WEAKNESSES OF
- narrow-mindedness
- over-critical
- over-analysis
- social awkwardness
- self-limiting boundaries
- lack of imagination
- lack of sensitivity
- lack of love

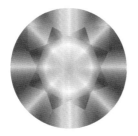

RUBY
ENERGY INFLUENCES OF RAY SIX
Astrological signs: *Virgo, Sagittarius, Pisces*

FAITH AND INSPIRATION
The essence of ruby focuses the sixth ray energies of devotion and idealism. Arouse inspired commitment and attain through one-pointed aspiration, fearlessness and endurance. The will to realise emotional health and intelligence stems from your awareness of, and influence over, instinctual orientations. With heartfelt devotion and a serene, sunny outlook on life, comes the power to excite, persuade and inspire.

SOUL

Virtues of the Ray
- devotion
- one-pointed aspiration
- love
- tenderness
- intuition
- loyalty
- humility
- self-sacrificial
- compassion
- purity
- the power to inspire

Virtues to be acquired
- tolerance
- purity
- truth
- serenity
- balance
- strength

MIND
- courage, bravery, fearlessness
- sunny outlook on life
- power to detach oneself, to dismiss that which is not desired
- master uncontrollable desires and passions
- will to remove anger and discord
- clear the mind of negative thoughts and bad dreams
- abate belittling or disparaging thoughts of yourself

BODY
- solar plexus *chakra*
- pancreas
- sympathetic nerves
- physical/etheric organs, systems and structures governed by the *chakra*
- problems and imbalances related to stomach, pancreas, liver, gall bladder and nervous system

POWER TO INTEGRATE WEAKNESSES OF
- fanaticism
- intolerance
- cynicism
- negative thoughts
- deception
- emotionalism
- being overly self-defensive
- martyr complex
- hyper-intensity

AMETHYST
ENERGY INFLUENCES OF RAY SEVEN
Astrological signs: *Aries, Cancer, Capricorn*

ORDER AND PRACTICALITY

The essence of amethyst focuses the seventh ray energies of order and organisation.

Manifest skill in action and bring order and organisation to all areas of living. Find the will to perfect expression through humility, wide-mindedness, perseverance and high intuition. Achieve through practicality and graceful, rhythmic activity. Discover the power to translate plans into physical reality through the magical work of interpretation and the synthesising ability.

SOUL

Virtues of the Ray

- the power to organise and manifest
- graceful activity
- courtesy
- perseverance
- courage
- independence
- individualism
- high intuition

Virtues to be acquired

- humility
- gentleness
- love
- realisation of unity
- wide-mindedness

MIND

- spiritual awareness and inner peace
- power to ward off unwanted external influences
- mental power
- intuition
- assimilate perceptions
- improved mental clarity
- strength to be who you truly are
- inner peace
- psychic insight
- stimulates third eye
- aids meditation and lucid dreaming

BODY

- *ajna chakra* (also base *chakra*)
- pituitary
- para-sympathetic nerves
- physical/etheric organs, systems and structures governed by the *chakra*
- problems and imbalances related to lower brain, eyes, ears, nose and nervous system

POWER TO INTEGRATE WEAKNESSES OF

- hyperactivity
- over-concern with rules and bureaucracy
- over-authoritarianism
- materialism
- excessive perfectionism
- disorderliness
- rebelliousness
- addiction to occult phenomena

Index

OF ATTRIBUTES AND INDICATIONS

ABANDONMENT
: Balsam, Rose Water Lily, Wintergreen
See also *Alienation, Loneliness, Rejection, Separation*

ABSENTMINDEDNESS
: **See** *Awareness, Confusion, Forgetfulness, Thinking/Thought Patterns*

ABUSE
: **See** *Addiction, Anger, Bullying, Co-dependence, Sexual abuse*

ABUNDANCE
: **See** *Prosperity*

ADOLESCENCE
: Daisy, Elder, Grass of Parnassus, Teens

ACCEPTANCE
: Cherry, Elf Cup Lichen, Holy Thorn, Lime, Rowan, Snowdrop, Spotted Orchid, Stonecrop, Wintergreen
See also Faith, Openness, Patience, Trust, Tolerance

ACTION
: Apple, Cabbage, Hazel, Laurel, Rose Alba, Thistle
See also *Energy, Goal, Motivation, Power, Vitality, Will*

ADDICTION
: Apple, Globethistle, Hazel, Iona Pennywort, Silverweed, Snowdrop, Spotted Orchid, Transformation, Watercress
See also *Denial, Co-dependence, Habit patterns, Obsession*

AGING
: Ginkgo, Elder, Sycamore
See also *Body, Energy, Rejuvenation, Self-esteem, Vitality*

AGGRESSION
: **See** *Anger, Bullying, Hostility*

ALIENATION
: Balsam, Cherry, Ginkgo, Gorse, Grass of Parnassus, Holy Thorn, Lime, Reindeer Lichen, Rose Water Lily, Snowdrop, Stonecrop
See also *Abandonment, Loneliness, Rejection, Separation*

ALIGNMENT
: Elecampane, Golden Iris, Harebell, Rose Alba, Clear Light, Holy Grail
See also *Attunement, Higher self, Spiritual connection*

ALOOFNESS	Balsam, Grass of Parnassus, Holy Thorn, Sea Holly **See also** *Loneliness, Shyness*
ALTRUISM	Globethistle, Exaltation, Holy Thorn, Wesak Blessing **See also** *Compassion, Unconditional love*
ANGER	Elf Cup Lichen, Monkey Flower, Rowan, Watercress, Willowherb **See also** *Hostility, Irritability, Resentment, Temper*
ANXIETY	Bell Heather, Daisy, Ginkgo, First Aid, Heart Support, Monkey Flower, Rose Water Lily, Scottish Primrose, Sea Holly, Thistle, Wild Pansy, Wintergreen **See also** *Confusion, Fear, Nervousness, Panic, Restlessness, Stress, Tension, Worry*
APATHY	Ginkgo, Gorse, Lady's Mantle **See also** *Energy, Fatigue, Laziness, Lethargy, Procrastination*
ASSERTIVENESS	Garden Pea, Monkey Flower, Scots Pine, Thistle **See also** *Action, Confidence, Courage, Empowerment, Motivation, Power, Strength, Will*
ATTENTION	Broom, Clear Light, Daisy, Ginkgo, Lady's Mantle, Spotted Orchid, Wild Pansy **See also** *Awareness, Concentration, Learning, Focus*
ATTUNEMENT	Broom, Elecampane, Golden Iris, Mallow, Rose Alba **See also** *Awareness, Comprehension, Higher self, Intuition, Knowledge, Meditation, Nature attunement, Perception, Receptivity, Sensitivity, Spiritual connection, Wisdom*
AUTHORITY	**See** *Assertiveness, Confidence, Control, Empowerment, Masculine principle, Power, Rebelliousness, Responsibility, Will*
AVOIDANCE	Apple, Elf Cup Lichen, Iona Pennywort **See also** *Apathy, Blocks, Denial, Laziness, Procrastination, Resistance*
AWARENESS	Birch, Clear Light, Elecampane, Ginkgo, Golden Iris, Gorse, Holy Grail, Iona Pennywort, Lady's Mantle, Laurel, Mallow, Sea Pink, Valerian, Willowherb, Wintergreen **See also** *Attunement, Clarity, Comprehension, Discrimination, Focus, Intuition, Knowledge, Light, Perception, Receptivity, Sensitivity, Thinking/Thought Patterns, Understanding*
BARRIERS	**See** *Blocks, Resistance*
BEREAVEMENT	**See** *Grief*
BIGOTED	**See** *Prejudice*
BIRTH AND BIRTHING	Balsam, Grass of Parnassus, Hazel, Holy Thorn, Stonecrop **See also** *Breakthrough, Bonding, Creativity, Feminine principle, Nurturing, Spiritual emergence, Transition*
BITTERNESS	**See** *Anger, Resentment, Hostility*
BLAME	Karma Clear, Rowan, Scottish Primrose **See also** *Criticism, Defensiveness, Guilt, Irritability, Resentment, Shame*
BLOCKS	Ancient Yew, Balsam, Cherry, Elf Cup Lichen, Garden Pea, Ginkgo, Hazel, Holy Thorn, Ragged Robin, Reindeer Lichen, Rose Water Lily, Rowan, Sea Holly, Sea Pink, Snowdrop, Stonecrop, Watercress, Wild Pansy **See also** *Avoidance, Resistance, Repression, Unconscious mind*

BODY	Balsam, Elder, Gorse, Ragged Robin, Reindeer Lichen, Scottish Primrose, Sycamore, Watercress **See also** *Flexibility, Intimacy, Male/female balance, Nurturing, Self-acceptance, Self-harm, Self-image, Sensitivity, Sexuality*
BONDING	Balsam, Cherry, Holy Thorn, Spiritual Marriage **See also** *Feminine principle, Love, Masculine principle, Nurturing, Relationship*
BOUNDARIES	**See** *Assertiveness*
BREAKTHROUGH	Ancient Yew, Hazel, Snowdrop, Stonecrop, Transformation **See also** *Birth and Birthing, Change, Crisis, Freedom, Spiritual emergence, Transition, Transformation*
BULLYING	Garden Pea, Monkey Flower, Rowan, Sea Holly, Willowherb **See also** *Hostility, Temper*
BURNOUT	**See** *Energy, Fatigue, Lethargy, Overwhelm*
CALM	Bell Heather, Daisy, Rose Water Lily, Scottish Primrose, Silverweed, Stonecrop, Thistle, Watercress, Wild Pansy, Willowherb, First Aid **See also** *Centering, Confidence, Control, Grounded, Patience, Peace, Relaxation, Security*
CATHARSIS	Elf Cup Lichen, Karma Clear, Ragged Robin, Watercress, Willowherb **See also** *Breakthrough, Cleansing, Release, Surrender*
CENTERING	Bell Heather, Daisy, First Aid, Scots Pine, Sea Pink, Valerian **See also** *Attunement, Calm, Confidence, Focus, Grounded, Security*
CHANGE	Ancient Yew, Bell Heather, Sea Rocket, Snowdrop, Stonecrop **See also** *Breakthrough, Spiritual emergence, Transition, Transformation*
CHANNELLING	**See** *Communication, Intuition, Higher self, Perception, Receptivity, Sensitivity, Spiritual connection*
CHILDHOOD	**See** *Birth and Birthing, Bonding, Inner Child, Nurturing, Relationship*
CLARITY	Birch, Broom, Clear Light, Garden Pea, Ginkgo, Laurel, Mallow, Scots Pine, Sea Rocket, Wild Pansy, Watercress **See also** *Attention, Awareness, Concentration, Decision, Light, Perception, Thinking/Thought Patterns, Understanding*
CLEANSING	Elf Cup Lichen, Go with the Flow, Reindeer Lichen, Watercress **See also** *Body, Catharsis, Release, Surrender, Transformation*
CO-DEPENDENCE	Globethistle, Karma Clear, Transformation **See also** *Addiction, Denial, Habit patterns, Obsession*
COMMITMENT	Apple, Cabbage, Laurel **See also** *Decision, Perseverance, Responsibility*
COMMUNICATION	Broom, Cherry, Clear Light, Elecampane, Garden Pea, Ginkgo, Lady's Mantle, Mallow, Rose Alba, Sea Holly, Voice Confidence **See also** *Awareness, Channelling, Clarity, Expression, Relationship, Speaking, Understanding*
COMPASSION	Cherry, Holy Thorn, Karma Clear, Lime, Scottish Primrose **See also** *Openness, Sensitivity, Tenderness, Tolerance, Unconditional love, Understanding*
COMPULSIVENESS	**See** *Obsession*
COMPREHENSION	Broom, Clear Light, Lady's Mantle **See also** *Attention, Awareness, Concentration, Clarity, Knowledge, Learning, Light, Perception, Thinking/Thought Patterns, Understanding*

CONCENTRATION	Broom, Cabbage, Clear Light, Daisy, Ginkgo, Golden Iris, Wild Pansy **See also** *Attention, Awareness, Clarity, Focus, Learning, Meditation, Thinking/Thought patterns*
CONFIDENCE	Bell Heather, Elder, Garden Pea, Harebell, Monkey Flower, Sea Holly, Scots Pine, Thistle, Voice Confidence **See also** *Assertiveness, Calm, Faith, Empowerment, Security, Trust*
CONFLICT	**See** *Crisis, Hostility, Stress, Tension*
CONFUSION	Birch, Broom, Daisy, Ginkgo, Lady's Mantle, Scots Pine, Sea Pink, Wild Pansy **See also** *Anxiety, Forgetfulness, Thinking/Thought patterns*
CONTROL	Bell Heather, Hazel, Sea Rocket, Willowherb **See also** *Calm, Power, Obstinate, Repression, Will*
COURAGE	First Aid, Harebell, Monkey Flower, Rose Water Lily, Sea Holly, Thistle, Voice Confidence, Wintergreen **See also** *Assertiveness, Confidence, Empowerment, Masculine Principle, Passion, Power, Protection, Strength, Trust, Will*
CRAVINGS	**See** *Addiction, Desire, Greed*
CREATIVITY	Fertility, Garden Pea, Holy Grail, Rose Alba, Sea Holly, Sea Rocket, Spotted Orchid, Voice Confidence **See also** *Confidence, Expression, Inspiration, Vision*
CRISIS	Bell Heather, First Aid, Scottish Primrose, Thistle, Wintergreen **See also** *Emergency, Fear, Spiritual emergence, Pain, Panic, Stress, Tension, Trauma*
CRITICISM	Garden Pea, Globethistle, Lime, Sea Holly, Spotted Orchid, Watercress, Willowherb **See also** *Blame, Hostility, Irritability, Judgemental, Negativity*
CYNICISM	**See** *Negativity, Suspiciousness*
DARKNESS	Ginkgo, Gorse, Iona Pennywort, Light Being, Rose Water Lily, Snowdrop, Wintergreen **See also** *Depression, Despair, Hopelessness, Shadow self, Spiritual emergence, Unconscious mind, Winter blues*
DAYDREAMING	**See** *Escapism, Illusion, Thinking/Thought Patterns*
DEATH AND DYING	Rose Water Lily, Snowdrop, Stonecrop, Wintergreen **See also** *Darkness, Grief, Heartache, Loss, Spiritual emergence, Transition*
DECISION	Broom, Ginkgo, Clear Light, Golden Iris Harebell, Mallow, Scots Pine **See also** *Action, Commitment, Purpose, Thinking/Thought Patterns, Will*
DEFENSIVENESS	Garden Pea, Lime, Rowan, Watercress **See also** *Anger, Blocks, Hostility, Resistance*
DEJECTION	**See** *Despair, Grief, Sadness*
DELUSION	Birch, Clear Light, Wild Pansy **See also** *Confusion, Illusion, Paranoia*
DENIAL	Clear Light, Elf Cup Lichen, Iona Pennywort **See also** *Addiction, Avoidance, Blocks, Control, Escapism, Repression, Resistance*
DEPENDENCE	**See** *Addiction, Co-dependence, Habit patterns*

DEPLETION	**See** *Blocks, Body, Energy, Life Force, Fatigue*
DEPRESSION	First Aid, Gorse, Light Being, Snowdrop, Wintergreen **See also** *Darkness, Despair, Grief, Heartache, Hopelessness, Mood swing, Sadness, Winter blues*
DESIRE	Ragged Robin, Sea Pink, Silverweed **See also** *Addiction, Enthusiasm, Intimacy, Love, Manifestation, Passion*
DESPAIR	First Aid, Light Being, Rose Water Lily, Snowdrop, Wintergreen **See also** *Darkness, Depression, Hopelessness, Negativity, Sadness*
DETACHMENT	**See** *Non-attachment, Relationship*
DETERMINATION	**See** *Motivation, Perseverance, Strength, Will*
DEVOTION	**See** *Commitment, Love, Unconditional love*
DISCIPLINE	Apple, Cabbage, Iona Pennywort, Ragged Robin, Rose Alba, Sea Rocket, Silverweed **See also** *Commitment, Control, Motivation, Perseverance, Strength, Will*
DISCERNMENT	**See** *Discrimination, Perception*
DISCRIMINATION	Elecampane, Ginkgo, Golden Iris, Iona Pennywort, Lime, Laurel, Ragged Robin, Scots Pine **See also** *Awareness, Decision, Illusion, Judgemental, Thinking/ Thought Patterns, Wisdom*
DISORIENTATION	**See** *Confusion*
DOUBT	**See** *Confusion, Decision, Suspiciousness*
DREAM AND DREAMING	Birch, Elecampane, Ginkgo, Iona Pennywort, Lady's Mantle **See also** *Nightmare, Out-of-body, Shadow self, Sleep patterns, Unconscious mind*
DUALITY	**See** *Polarity*
EGOTISTIC	**See** *Selfishness*
EMERGENCY	Bell Heather, First Aid, Scottish Primrose, Thistle **See also** *Crisis, Fear, Pain, Panic, Shock, Stress, Trauma*
EMPOWERMENT	Garden Pea, Golden Iris, Laurel, Monkey Flower, Rose Alba, Scots Pine, Sea Holly, Thistle **See also** *Action, Confidence, Courage, Power, Strength, Will*
ENDURANCE	**See** *Strength*
ENERGY	Elder, Gorse, Life Force, Sea Pink, Sea Rocket, Sycamore, Wild Pansy **See also** *Action, Enthusiasm, Life Force, Vitality, Motivation, Passion, Power, Strength, Vitality, Will*
ENTHUSIASM	Apple, Cabbage, Gorse, Life Force, Valerian **See also** *Desire, Energy, Joy, Life Force, Lightness, Motivation, Passion, Vitality*
ENVY	**See** *Jealousy*
EXHAUSTION	**See** *Fatigue*
EXPRESSION	Garden Pea, Holy Thorn, Monkey Flower, Rose Alba, Sea Holly **See also** *Confidence, Creativity, Speaking*

FAITH	Bell Heather, Harebell, Rose Water Lily, Sea Rocket **See also** *Confidence, Hope, Optimism, Trust*
FANATICISM	**See** *Passion, Obsession*
FATHER	**See** *Masculine principle*
FATIGUE	Cabbage, Elder, Gorse, Life Force, Sea Pink, Sycamore, Valerian, Watercress **See also** *Energy, Lethargy*
FEAR	Iona Pennywort, First Aid, Monkey Flower, Scottish Primrose, Thistle, Wild Pansy, Wintergreen **See also** Anxiety, Confusion, Nervousness, Nightmare, Rigidity, Panic, Paranoia, Worry
FEMININE PRINCIPLE	Balsam, Grass of Parnassus, Fertility, Femininity, Holy-Grail, Sea Rocket **See also** *Birth and Birthing, Fertility, Male/Female balance,* *Nurturing, Sexuality*
FERTILITY	Balsam, Fertility, Grass of Parnassus, Holy Thorn, Sea Rocket **See also** *Birth and Birthing, Creativity, Feminine principle,* *Masculine principle*
FLEXIBILITY	Bell Heather, Cherry, Globethistle, Go With the Flow, Hazel, Ragged Robin, Rose Alba, Sycamore **See also** *Body, Openness*
FOCUS	Apple, Birch, Broom, Cabbage, Lady's Mantle, Laurel **See also** *Attention, Concentration, Learning, Thinking/Thought* *Patterns*
FORGETFULNESS	Broom, Clear Light, Daisy, Ginkgo **See also** *Confusion, Memory, Thinking/Thought Patterns*
FORGIVENESS	Holy Thorn, Karma Clear, Reindeer Lichen, Rowan **See also** *Acceptance, Compassion, Openness, Reconciliation,* *Unconditional love, Understanding*
FREEDOM	Ancient Yew, Globethistle, Hazel, Stonecrop **See also** *Breakthrough, Change, Release, Transformation*
FRUSTRATION	Elf Cup Lichen, Garden Pea, Spotted Orchid, Stonecrop, Sycamore
FUSSINESS	**See** *Habit patterns, Obsession*
GOAL	Ancient Yew, Apple, Cabbage, Harebell, Laurel **See also** *Desire, Manifestation, Purpose*
GREED	**See** *Addiction, Desire, Materialism, Selfishness*
GRIEF	First Aid, Reindeer Lichen, Rowan, Scottish Primrose, Snowdrop, Wintergreen **See also** *Death and dying, Despair, Heartache, Loss, Pain,* *Pining Sadness, Separation*
GROUNDING	Bell Heather, Daisy, Elecampane, Ginkgo, Harebell, Iona Pennywort, Rose Water Lily, Scottish Primrose, Sea Pink, Silverweed, Thistle, First Aid **See also** *Calm, Centering, Control, Security*
GUILT	Elf Cup Lichen, Globethistle, Iona Pennywort, Karma Clear, Scots Pine **See also** *Blame, Criticism, Shame*

HABIT PATTERNS	Ancient Yew, Elf Cup Lichen, Globethistle, Iona Pennywort, Ragged Robin, Sea Rocket, Silverweed, Transformation, Valerian, Watercress
	See also *Addiction, Blocks, Denial, Obsession, Unconscious mind*
HAPPINESS	**See** *Joy, Playfulness*
HEARTACHE	Cherry, Gorse, Grass of Parnassus, Reindeer Lichen, Rose Water Lily, Scottish Primrose, Wintergreen
	See also *Despair, Grief, Loneliness, Pain, Pining, Sadness, Separation, Transition*
HIGHER SELF	Clear Light, Elecampane, Monkey Flower, Rose Alba, Rose Water Lily, Wintergreen
	See also *Attunement, Intuition, Meditation, Perception, Receptivity, Spiritual connection, Wisdom*
HOARDING	**See** *Addiction, Compulsiveness, Obsession*
HOLDING ON	**See** *Blocks, Denial, Control, Repression, Resistance, Stagnation*
HOMESICKNESS	**See** *Pining*
HONESTY	**See** *Openness, Truth*
HOPE	**See** *Confidence, Faith, Optimism, Trust*
HOPELESSNESS	Gorse, Light Being, Reindeer Lichen, Snowdrop
	See also *Darkness, Depression, Despair, Grief, Heartache, Sadness*
HOSTILITY	Cherry, Lime, Karma Clear, Rowan, Willlowherb
	See also *Anger, Defensiveness, Rebelliousness, Resentment*
HYSTERIA	Daisy, First Aid, Scottish Primrose
	See also *Mood swing, Obsession, Panic, Passion*
ILLUSION	Birch, Broom, Elecampane, Iona Pennywort
	See also *Confusion, Delusion, Escapism*
IMAGINATION	**See** *Creativity, Inspiration, Intuition, Perception, Thinking/Thought Patterns, Vision*
IMPATIENCE	**See** *Anxiety, Frustration, Irritability, Nervousness, Patience, Restlessness*
IMMUNITY	Elder, Gorse, Life Force, Sycamore, Watercress
	See also *Protection, Resistance, Security, Strength*
INDECISION	**See** *Confusion, Decision, Doubt*
INFERIORITY	Bell Heather, Garden Pea, Monkey Flower, Sea Holly
	See also *Blocks, Self-empowerment, Self-image, Shyness, Unsociable*
INFLEXIBILITY	**See** *Rigidity*
INNER CHILD	Daisy, Elder, Garden Pea, Grass of Parnassus, Inner Child, Monkey Flower, Sea Holly, Valerian
	See also *Openness, Playfulness, Vulnerability*
INSECURITY	Daisy, Garden Pea, Gorse, Grass of Parnassus, Harebell, Lady's Mantle, Lime, Monkey Flower, Scots Pine, Sea Holly, Sea Rocket, Spotted Orchid, Thistle, Wild Pansy, Wintergreen
INSPIRATION	Birch, Broom, Clear Light, Golden Iris, Holy Grail, Laurel, Rose Alba
	See also *Creativity, Intuition, Light, Receptivity, Universal mind, Vision, Wisdom*

INTEGRATION	Ginkgo, Golden Iris, Elf Cup Lichen, Holy Grail, Iona Pennywort, Lady's Mantle, Reindeer Lichen, Sea Pink, Spiritual Marriage, Willowherb
INTELLIGENCE	See *Clarity, Comprehension, Knowledge, Light, Thinking/Thought Patterns, Understanding*
INTIMACY	Balsam, Eros, Grass of Parnassus, Spiritual Marriage See also *Body, Desire, Love, Nurturing, Openness, Relationship, Sensitivity, Sexuality, Tenderness, Trust*
INTOLERANCE	Cherry, Holy Thorn, Lime, Watercress, Willowherb
INTUITION	Broom, Clear Light, Elecampane, Golden Iris, Laurel, Mallow, Rose Alba, Scots Pine See also *Attunement, Awareness, Higher self, Inspiration, Knowledge, Light, Meditation, Perception, Receptivity, Sensitivity, Spiritual connection, Universal mind, Wisdom*
IRRITABILITY	Cherry, Elf Cup Lichen, Globethistle, Lime, Monkey Flower, Rowan, Seasonal Affections, Willowherb, Watercress See also *Anger, Criticism, Hostility, Mood swing, Negativity, Temper*
ISOLATION	See *Alienation, Loneliness*
JEALOUSY	See also *Suspiciousness*
JOY	Elder, Gorse, Valerian See also *Light, Lightness, Love, Playfulness*
JUDGEMENTAL	Cherry, Iona Pennywort, Karma Clear, Lime, Rowan See also *Criticism, Discrimination, Negativity*
KARMA	Ancient Yew, Cherry, Elf Cup Lichen, Karma Clear, Rowan See also *Action, Awareness, Discrimination, Understanding*
KNOWLEDGE	Broom, Elecampane, Lady's Mantle See also *Comprehension, Learning, Thinking/Thought Patterns, Understanding, Universal mind, Wisdom*
KUNDALINI ENERGY	See *Energy, Higher self, Spiritual emergence*
LAZINESS	See *Avoidance, Lethargy, Procrastination, Resistance*
LEADERSHIP	Cabbage, Laurel, Rose Alba See also *Assertiveness, Control, Courage, Decision, Empowerment, Motivation, Responsibility, Power*
LEARNING	Broom, Clear Light, Lady's Mantle See also *Attention, Clarity, Comprehension, Concentration, Focus, Knowledge, Light, Thinking/Thought Patterns, Understanding*
LETHARGY	Apple, Cabbage, Elder, Gorse, Life Force, Sycamore See also *Apathy, Energy, Fatigue, Laziness*
LETTING GO	See also *Blocks, Catharsis, Release, Surrender*
LIFE FORCE	Elder, Ginkgo, Gorse, Life Force, Ragged Robin, Reindeer Lichen, Sea Pink Sycamore, Wild Pansy See also *Energy, Immunity, Power, Strength, Vitality*
LIGHT	Ginkgo, Golden Iris, Gorse, Grass of Parnassus, Iona Pennywort, Rose Water Lily, Snowdrop, Wintergreen, Clear Light See also *Awareness, Comprehension, Inspiration, Intuition, Knowledge, Radiance, Understanding, Vision*
LIFE PURPOSE	See *Purpose*

LIGHTNESS	Elder, Gorse, Light Being, Silverweed, Snowdrop, Sycamore, Valerian **See also** *Joy, Relaxation*
LONELINESS	Elf Cup Lichen, Grass of Parnassus, Rose Water Lily, Stonecrop **See also** *Abandonment, Alienation, Loneliness, Separation*
LOSS	Heart Support, Reindeer Lichen, Rose Water Lily, Snowdrop **See also** *Death and dying, Grief, Heartache, Loneliness, Pining, Sadness*
LOVE	Balsam, Holy-Grail, Holy Thorn, Grass of Parnassus, Rose Water Lily, Scottish Primrose **See also** *Compassion, Intimacy, Openness, Relationship, Self-love, Tenderness, Unconditional love, Understanding*
LOVESICKNESS	**See** *Heartache, Pining*
MALE / FEMALE BALANCE	Eros, Cherry, Mallow, Spiritual Marriage **See also** *Bonding, Feminine principle, Masculine principle, Relationship*
MANIA	**See** *Fanaticism, Hysteria, Mood swing, Obsession, Passion, Panic*
MANIFESTATION	Cabbage, Harebell, Laurel, Prosperity, Sea Rocket **See also** *Desire, Goal, Prosperity, Purpose, Thought/Thought patterns*
MANIPULATION	**See** *Controlling, Power, Will*
MARTYR	**See** *Victim*
MASCULINE PRINCIPLE	Cherry, Masculinity, Rose Alba, Spiritual Marriage **See also** *Action, Courage, Male/female balance, Power, Sexuality, Strength, Will*
MATERIALISM	Laurel, Sea Rocket, Silverweed, Spotted Orchid, Watercress **See also** *Desire, Obsessive, Possessiveness*
MEDITATION	**See** *Attunement, Clarity, Concentration, Higher self, Intuition, Perception, Receptivity, Spiritual connection, Universal mind, Wisdom*
MELANCHOLY	**See** *Sadness*
MEMORY	Ancient Yew, Broom, Clear Light, Ginkgo, Lady's Mantle **See also** *Forgetfulness, Thinking/Thought Patterns*
MENTAL CLARITY	**See** *Attention, Awareness, Clarity, Comprehension, Concentration, Focus, Thinking/Thought Patterns*
MIASMS	**See** *Karma*
MOOD SWING	Daisy, Sea Rocket, Watercress, Willowherb **See also** *Anxiety, Depression, Irritability, Hysteria, Stress, Tension*
MOTHER	**See** *Feminine Principle*
MOTIVATION	Apple, Cabbage, Elecampane, Garden Pea, Gorse, Laurel **See also** *Action, Commitment, Empowerment, Energy, Enthusiasm, Passion, Power, Purpose, Will*
NATURE, ATTUNEMENT	**See** *Attunement, Higher Self, Intuition, Meditation, Perception, Receptivity, Spiritual connection, Wisdom*
NEGATIVITY	Cherry, Garden Pea, Harebell, Lime, Rowan, Snowdrop, Spotted Orchid **See also** *Criticism, Depression, Despair, Hopelessness*

NERVOUSNESS	Daisy, First Aid, Grass of Parnassus, Monkey Flower, Scottish Primrose, Sea Holly, Sycamore, Valerian, Wild Pansy **See also** *Anxiety, Fear, Panic, Restlessness, Shyness, Stress, Tension, Worry*
NIGHTMARE	Ginkgo, Iona Pennywort, Lady's Mantle, Snowdrop **See also** *Anxiety, Dream and dreaming, Fear, Illusion, Shadow self, Sleep patterns, Unconscious mind*
NON-ATTACHMENT	Ancient Yew, Globethistle, Golden Iris, Hazel, Silverweed, Snowdrop, Stonecrop **See also** *Awareness, Desire, Flexibility*
NOSTALGIA	**See** *Pining*
NURTURING	Balsam, Elder, Holy Thorn, Sea Rocket **See also** *Body, Feminine principle, Self-acceptance, Self-image, Self-love*
OBSESSION	Iona Pennywort, Ragged Robin, Silverweed, Spotted Orchid **See also** *Addiction, Compulsiveness, Fanaticism, Habit patterns, Hysteria, Passion*
OBSTINATE	Cherry, Hazel, Rowan, Silverweed, Spotted Orchid, Willowherb **See also** *Blocks, Holding on, Resistance, Rigidity*
OPENNESS	Balsam, Cherry, Daisy, Grass of Parnassus, Holy Thorn, Sea Holly, Valerian, Wild Pansy **See also** *Acceptance, Flexibility, Inner Child, Receptivity, Sensitivity, Tolerance, Trust, Understanding, Vulnerability*
OPTIMISM	Gorse, Harebell, Snowdrop, Spotted Orchid, Wintergreen **See also** *Confidence, Enthusiasm, Faith, Trust*
OUT-OF-BODY	Balsam, Daisy, Lady's Mantle, Rose Water Lily, Scottish Primrose **See also** *Shock, Sleep patterns, Spiritual emergence, Trauma*
OVERWHELM	Daisy, Lady's Mantle, Sea Pink **See also** *Stress, Tension, Workaholic, Worry*
PAIN	First Aid, Karma Clear, Rowan, Reindeer Lichen, Scottish Primrose, Snowdrop, Wintergreen **See also** *Crisis, Emergency, Grief, Heartache, Sadness, Shock, Stress, Tension*
PANIC	First Aid, Heart Support, Scottish Primrose, Thistle, Wild Pansy **See also** *Anxiety, Fear, Hysteria, Nervousness, Obsession, Overwhelm*
PARANOIA	**See also** *Fear, Delusion, Obsession, Worry*
PARENTING	**See** *Bonding, Nurturing*
PASSION	Apple, Balsam, Gorse, Willowherb **See also** *Desire, Courage, Enthusiasm, Love, Mania*
PATIENCE	Balsam, Globethistle, Rose Alba, Spotted orchid, Stonecrop, Valerian, Willowherb, Wintergreen **See also** *Calm, Perseverance, Tolerance, Understanding*
PEACE	Lime, Rose Water Lily, Scottish Primrose **See also** *Calm, Centering, Relaxation*
PERCEPTION	Birch, Clear Light, Elecampane, Golden Iris, Lady's Mantle **See also** *Awareness, Comprehension, Discrimination, Intuition, Knowledge, Receptivity, Thinking/Thought Patterns, Understanding, Vision*

PERFECTIONISM	Elder, Ragged Robin, Scots Pine, Silverweed, Spotted Orchid **See also** *Control, Fanaticism, Obsession*
PERSEVERANCE	Apple, Bell Heather, Cabbage, Ginkgo, Globethistle, Harebell, Laurel, Rose Alba, Sea Rocket, Stonecrop **See also** *Commitment, Discipline, Motivation, Patience, Strength, Will*
PESSIMISM	**See** *Negativity*
PINING	Reindeer Lichen, Rose Water Lily, Snowdrop **See also** *Grief, Heartache, Sadness, Separation*
PLAYFULNESS	Daisy, Inner Child, Valerian **See also** *Inner Child, Joy, Light, Lightness*
POLARITY	Cherry, Golden Iris, Iona Pennywort, Mallow, Sea Pink, Spiritual Marriage
POSITIVITY	**See** *Optimism*
POSSESSIVENESS	**See** *Desire, Jealous, Materialism, Obsession*
POWER	Apple, Monkey Flower, Rose Alba, Thistle, Willowherb **See also** *Action, Assertiveness, Courage, Empowerment, Energy, Life force, Masculine principle, Motivation, Responsibility, Strength, Vitality, Will*
PREJUDICE	**See** *Criticism, Discrimination, Judgemental, Hostility*
PROCRASTINATION	Apple, Cabbage, Hazel, Laurel **See also** *Apathy, Avoidance, Blocks, Laziness, Lethargy, Resistance*
PROSPERITY	Harebell, Laurel, Prosperity, Sea Rocket **See also** *Manifestation*
PROTECTION	Daisy, Energy Shield, First Aid, Grass of Parnassus, Psychic Protection, Thistle, Watercress **See also** *Centering, Courage, Strength, Power, Security, Vitality*
PUBERTY	**See** *Adolescence*
PUBLIC SPEAKING	**See** *Speaking*
PURIFICATION	**See** *Cleansing*
PURPOSE	Ancient Yew, Apple, Cabbage, Clear Light, Laurel, Rose Alba, Wintergreen **See also** *Alignment, Commitment, Goal, Higher self, Motivation, Strength, Will*
RAGE	**See** *Anger, Hysteria, Obsession, Passion, Panic*
REBELLIOUSNESS	**See** *Adolescence, Alienation, Hostility, Irritability*
RECEPTIVITY	Clear Light, Elecampane, Grass of Parnassus, Mallow, Sea Pink, Wild Pansy **See also** *Openness, Flexibility, Sensitivity, Tolerance*
RECONCILIATION	Cherry, Karma Clear, Lime, Mallow, Rowan, Scottish Primrose, Spiritual Marriage **See also** *Acceptance, Compassion, Forgiveness, Unconditional love, Understanding*
REJECTION	Balsam, Grass of Parnassus, Holy Thorn, Sea Holly **See also** *Abandonment, Alienation, Loneliness, Separation*
REJUVENATION	Elder, Life Force, Sea Rocket, Sycamore Energy, Life Force, Vitality

RELATIONSHIP	Ancient Yew, Balsam, Cabbage, Cherry, Eros, Gorse, Grass of Parnassus, Holy Thorn, Lime, Mallow, Reindeer Lichen, Rowan, Scottish Primrose, Sea Holly, Sea Pink, Spiritual Marriage **See also** *Bonding, Communication, Intimacy, Love, Spiritual connection, Unconditional love*
RELAXATION	Gorse, Hazel, Scottish Primrose, Sycamore, Valerian **See also** *Body, Calm, Flexibility, Lightness, Nurturing, Peace*
RELEASE	Ancient Yew, Elf Cup Lichen, Hazel, Karma Clear, Ragged Robin, Reindeer Lichen, Snowdrop, Stonecrop, Transformation, Wintergreen **See also** *Breakthrough, Catharsis, Cleansing, Release, Surrender*
REMORSE	**See** *Guilt, Shame*
REPRESSION	Balsam, Elf Cup Lichen, Garden Pea, Grass of Parnassus, Holy Thorn, Iona Pennywort, Monkey Flower, Ragged Robin, Reindeer Lichen, Rowan, Sea Holly **See also** *Avoidance, Blocks, Denial, Control, Resistance, Unconscious mind*
RESENTMENT	Cherry, Globethistle, Karma Clear, Rowan **See also** *Anger, Blame, Hostility, Irritability, Jealousy*
RESISTANCE	Apple, Elf Cup Lichen, Hazel, Reindeer Lichen, Stonecrop, Snowdrop, Karma Clear, Watercress, Wild Pansy **See also** *Avoidance, Blocks, Holding on, Obstinate, Tension*
RESPONSIBILITY	Apple, Globethistle, Laurel, Lime, Rose Alba **See also** *Control, Leadership, Power*
RESTLESSNESS	Ginkgo, Hazel, Rose Water Lily, Stonecrop, Valerian, Wild Pansy **See also** *Nervousness, Tension*
RIGIDITY	Cherry, Globethistle, Hazel, Lime, Ragged Robin, Rose Alba, Rowan, Silverweed **See also** *Fear, Holding on, Obstinate, Resistance, Stagnation, Tension*
SABOTAGE	**See** *Self-sabotage*
SADNESS	Grass of Parnassus, Heart Support, Reindeer Lichen, Rose Water Lily, Snowdrop, Spotted Orchid, Wintergreen **See also** *Depression, Despair, Grief, Heartache*
SAFETY	**See** *Protection, Security, Sensitivity*
SECURITY	Bell Heather, Grass of Parnassus, Harebell, Psychic Protection **See also** *Calm, Confidence, Immunity, Peace, Protection, Sensitivity, Trust*
SELF-ACCEPTANCE	Elder, Harebell, Holy Thorn, Iona Pennywort, Monkey Flower, Spotted Orchid **See also** *Acceptance, Body, Male/female balance, Nurturing, Self-confidence, Self-esteem, Self-image, Self-love, Tolerance*
SELF-CENTRED	**See** *Selfishness*
SELF-CONFIDENCE	**See** *Confidence*
SELF-CONTROL	**See** *Discipline*
SELF-CRITICISM	Elder, Holy Thorn, Ragged Robin, Scots Pine, Spotted Orchid
SELF-DISCIPLINE	**See** *Discipline*

SELF-EMPOWERMENT	**See** *Empowerment*
SELF-ESTEEM	Elder, Garden Pea, Monkey Flower, Scots Pine **See also** *Confidence, Self-acceptance, Self-love*
SELF-EXPRESSION	**See** *Expression*
SELF-HARM	Balsam, Elder, Holy Thorn, Ragged Robin **See also** *Body, Self-acceptance, Self-image, Self-love*
SELF-IMAGE	Elder, Garden Pea, Harebell, Iona Pennywort, Ragged Robin, Sea Holy **See also** *Body, Male/female balance, Self-esteem, Self-love*
SELFLESSNESS	**See** *Awareness, Compassion, Unconditional love, Understanding*
SELF-LOVE	Balsam, Harebell, Holy Thorn, Lime, Scots Pine **See also** *Acceptance, Love, Nurturing, Self-acceptance, Self-esteem, Self-image, Unconditional love*
SELF-MASTERY	**See** *Calm, Centering, Confidence, Control, Discipline*
SELF-PITY	Globethistle, Ragged Robin, Rowan
SELF-REALISATION	Golden Iris, Monkey Flower, Reindeer Lichen, Silverweed
SELF-SABOTAGE	Garden Pea, Globethistle, Iona Pennywort, Laurel, Spotted Orchid
SELF-WORTH	**See** *Self-esteem*
SELFISHNESS	**See** *Greed, Self-centred*
SENSITIVITY	Balsam, Cherry, Elecampane, Garden Pea, Grass of Parnassus, Lady's Mantle, Psychic Protection, Sea Holly, Valerian **See also** *Awareness, Compassion, Openness, Protection, Receptivity, Tenderness, Understanding, Vulnerability*
SENSUALITY	Balsam, Elder, Eros **See also** *Body, Intimacy, Nurturing, Sensitivity, Sexuality, Tenderness*
SEPARATION	Balsam, Gorse, Lime, Mallow, Rose Water Lily, Scottish Primrose, Sea Pink, Sea Rocket, Snowdrop, Stonecrop, Spiritual Marriage, Wild Pansy, Wintergreen **See also** *Abandonment, Alienation, Loneliness, Relationship*
SEXUALITY	Balsam, Eros, Rose Alba, Sea Pink, Sexual Integrity **See also** *Body, Intimacy, Love, Feminine principle, Intimacy, Male/ Female balance, Masculine principle, Nurturing, Openness, Sensitivity, Sensuality, Tenderness, Vulnerability*
SEXUAL ABUSE	Daisy, First Aid, Elf Cup Lichen, Karma Clear, Sexual Integrity **See also** *Anxiety, Despair, Fear, Guilt, Shame*
SHADOW SELF	Elf Cup Lichen, Iona Pennywort, Sea Rocket, Wintergreen **See also** *Darkness, Repression, Unconscious mind*
SHAME	Elf Cup Lichen, Iona Pennywort, Rowan, Sea Holly **See also** *Blame, Criticism, Guilt*
SHOCK	Bell Heather, Daisy, First Aid, Scottish Primrose, Thistle **See also** *Confusion, Crisis, Emergency, Trauma*
SHYNESS	Daisy, Elder, Monkey Flower, Sea Holly **See also** *Fear, Inferiority, Nervousness*

SLEEP PATTERNS	Ginkgo, Lady's Mantle, Scottish Primrose, Sweet Dreams **See also** *Dream, Nightmare, Unconscious mind*
SOOTHING	First Aid, Grass of Parnassus, Scottish Primrose, Sycamore
SOUL	**See** *Attunement, Awareness, Higher Self, Intuition, Meditation, Spiritual connection*
SPEAKING	Clear Light, Garden Pea, Holy Thorn, Lady's Mantle, Mallow, Rose Alba, Sea Holly, Voice Confidence **See also** *Confidence, Creativity, Expression*
SPIRITUAL CONNECTION	Cabbage, Elecampane, Golden Iris, Rose Water Lily, Clear Light, Holy Grail, Wintergreen **See also** *Attunement, Channelling, Higher self, Inspiration, Intuition, Meditation, Receptivity, Sensitivity, Universal mind, Wisdom*
SPIRITUAL EMERGENCE	Golden Iris, Rose Water Lily, Wintergreen **See also** *Alienation, Birth and Birthing, Breakthrough, Darkness, Despair, Separation, Transition, Transformation*
STAGNATION	Hazel, Stonecrop, Watercress **See also** *Blocks, Holding on, Resistance, Rigidity*
STRENGTH	Bell Heather, Cabbage, Elecampane, Globethistle, Harebell, Life Force, Rose Water Lily, Snowdrop, Sycamore, Thistle, Wintergreen **See also** *Courage, Flexibility, Life force, Power, Vitality, Will*
STRESS	Bell Heather, Daisy, First Aid, Rose Water Lily, Sycamore, Thistle, Valerian, Wintergreen **See also** *Anxiety, Nervousness, Shock, Tension, Worry*
STUBBORN	**See** *Control, Obstinate, Rigidity*
STUCK	**See** *Blocks, Stagnation, Resistance*
SURRENDER	Ancient Yew, Hazel, Reindeer Lichen, Rose Water Lily, Snowdrop, Wintergreen **See also** *Release*
SUSPICIOUSNESS	**See** *Fear, Delusion, Obsession, Paranoia*
TANTRUMS	**See** *Temper*
TEENS	**See** *Adolescence*
TEMPER	Globe Thistle, Watercress, Willowherb **See also** *Anger, Hysteria, Irritability, Negativity*
TENDERNESS	Balsam, Cherry, Grass of Parnassus, Holy Thorn **See also** *Compassion, Intimacy, Love, Openness, Sensitivity, Sensuality, Understanding*
TENSION	Cherry, First Aid, Rowan, Scottish Primrose, Sycamore, Valerian, Wild Pansy, Wintergreen **See also** *Anxiety, Hostility, Nervousness, Restlessness, Rigidity, Shock, Stress, Worry*
TERROR	**See** *Fear*
THINKING/THOUGHT PATTERNS	Birch, Broom, Ginkgo, Golden Iris, Hazel, Harebell, Lime, Laurel, Mallow, Ragged Robin, Scots Pine, Spotted Orchid, Watercress **See also** *Attention, Awareness, Clarity, Comprehension, Concentration, Decision, Discrimination, Illusion, Imagination, Knowledge, Learning, Understanding*

TIREDNESS	**See** *Energy, Fatigue, Lethargy*
TOLERANCE	Globethistle, Holy Thorn, Lime, Rowan, Spotted Orchid, Sycamore **See also** *Acceptance, Compassion, Openness, Patience,* *Understanding, Unconditional love*
TRANSFORMATION	Ancient Yew, Grass of Parnassus, Stonecrop, Transformation, Reindeer Lichen, Watercress **See also** *Change, Transition*
TRANSITION	Go With the Flow, Hazel, Snowdrop, Stonecrop, Transformation **See also** *Birth and Birthing, Change, Death and Dying,* *Transformation*
TRANSMUTATION	**See** *Change, Transition, Transformation*
TRAUMA	Bell Heather, Daisy, First Aid, Scottish Primrose, Thistle **See also** *Anxiety, Crisis, Emergency, Grief, Heartache, Pain, Shock,* *Stress, Tension*
TRUTH	**See** *Knowledge, Universal mind, Wisdom*
TRUST	Bell Heather, Grass of Parnassus, Harebell, Hazel, Lime, Scots Pine, Sea Holy, Sea Rocket, Silverweed, Snowdrop **See also** *Acceptance, Confidence, Faith, Protection, Security*
UNCONDITIONAL LOVE	Cherry, Exaltation, Holy Thorn, Rowan, Scottish Primrose **See also** *Acceptance, Compassion, Love, Openness, Tenderness,* *Tolerance, Trust*
UNCONSCIOUS MIND	Elf Cup Lichen, Iona Pennywort, Lady's Mantle **See also** *Dream and dreaming, Shadow self,* *Sleep and sleep patterns, Repression*
UNDERSTANDING	Birch, Cherry, Golden Iris, Holy Thorn, Lady's Mantle, Rowan, Scots Pine, Scottish Primrose **See also** *Awareness, Clarity, Comprehension, Compassion,* *Knowledge, Learning, Light, Openness, Patience, Thinking/Thought* *Patterns, Tolerance, Wisdom*
UNIVERSAL MIND	Birch, Clear Light, Scots Pine, Wesak Blessing **See also** *Higher self, Knowledge, Inspiration, Intuition, Perception,* *Spiritual connection, Wisdom*
UNSOCIABLE	**See** *Aloofness, Inferiority, Shyness*
VICTIM	Garden Pea, Globethistle, Monkey Flower, Rowan, Sea Rocket
VIOLENCE	**See** *Anger, Irritability, Hostility*
VISION	Birch, Cabbage, Clear Light, Elecampane, Golden Iris, Laurel **See also** *Creativity, Imagination, Inspiration, Intuition, Light,* *Manifestation, Perception*
VITALITY	Cabbage, Gorse, Elder, Life Force, Sea Pink, Sycamore **See also** *Action, Energy, Enthusiasm, Force, Passion, Power,* *Strength, Rejuvenation*
VULNERABILITY	Daisy, Grass of Parnassus, Sea Holly, Thistle **See also** *Grounded, Inner Child, Openness, Protection, Security,* *Sensitivity, Trust*
WILL	Ancient Yew, Apple, Cabbage, Elecampane, Harebell, Laurel, Rose Alba, Spotted Orchid, Stonecrop, Thistle, Willowherb **See also** *Action, Commitment, Courage, Discipline,* *Masculine principle, Motivation, Power, Purpose, Strength, Vitality*

WINTER BLUES Baby Blues, Ginkgo, Gorse, Light Being, Seasonal Affections, Snowdrop
See *Darkness, Depression*

WISDOM Clear Light, Elecampane, Golden Iris, Holy Grail, Laurel, Mallow, Scots Pine, Wesak Blessing
See also *Awareness, Inspiration, Intuition, Knowledge, Perception, Understanding, Universal mind, Vision*

WITHDRAWN See *Alienation, Aloofness, Loneliness, Shyness, Unsociable*

WORKAHOLIC Cabbage, Globethistle, Spotted Orchid, Sycamore, Valerian
See also *Addiction, Fanaticism, Habit patterns, Obsession, Passion*

WORRY Birch, Scots Pine, Spotted Orchid, Valerian, Wild Pansy
See also *Anxiety, Fear, Nervousness, Panic, Paranoia, Restlessness, Stress, Tension*

WRITING Broom, Clear Light, Mallow, Rose Alba
See also *Creativity, Expression, Imagination, Inspiration*

Dowsing Charts

POSITION THE PENDULUM WITH THE POINT ON THE SMALL HALF CIRCLE ON THE BOTTOM EDGE OF THE CHART. ON THE FULL CIRCLE CHART, POSITION THE POINT OF THE PENDULUM IN THE CENTRE.

FLOWERS ESSENCES

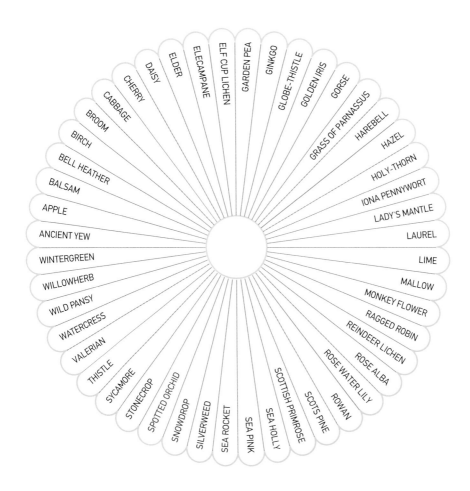

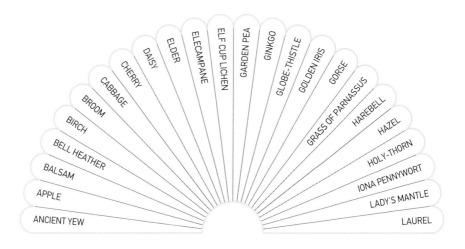

ANCIENT YEW
APPLE
BALSAM
BELL HEATHER
BIRCH
BROOM
CABBAGE
CHERRY
DAISY
ELDER
ELECAMPANE
ELF CUP LICHEN
GARDEN PEA
GINKGO
GLOBE-THISTLE
GOLDEN IRIS
GORSE
GRASS OF PARNASSUS
HAREBELL
HAZEL
HOLY-THORN
IONA PENNYWORT
LADY'S MANTLE
LAUREL

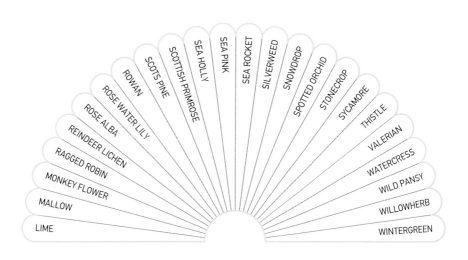

LIME
MALLOW
MONKEY FLOWER
RAGGED ROBIN
REINDEER LICHEN
ROSE ALBA
ROSE WATER LILY
ROWAN
SCOTS PINE
SCOTTISH PRIMROSE
SEA HOLLY
SEA PINK
SEA ROCKET
SILVERWEED
SNOWDROP
SPOTTED ORCHID
STONECROP
SYCAMORE
THISTLE
VALERIAN
WATERCRESS
WILD PANSY
WILLOWHERB
WINTERGREEN

COMBINATION ESSENCES

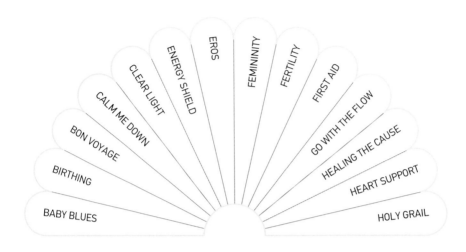

BABY BLUES
BIRTHING
BON VOYAGE
CALM ME DOWN
CLEAR LIGHT
ENERGY SHIELD
EROS
FEMININITY
FERTILITY
FIRST AID
GO WITH THE FLOW
HEALING THE CAUSE
HEART SUPPORT
HOLY GRAIL

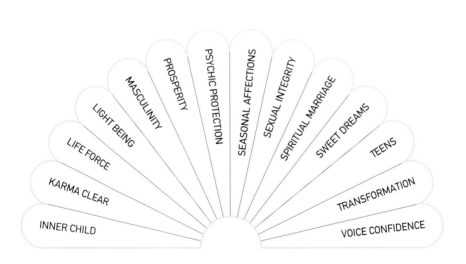

INNER CHILD
KARMA CLEAR
LIFE FORCE
LIGHT BEING
MASCULINITY
PROSPERITY
PSYCHIC PROTECTION
SEASONAL AFFECTIONS
SEXUAL INTEGRITY
SPIRITUAL MARRIAGE
SWEET DREAMS
TEENS
TRANSFORMATION
VOICE CONFIDENCE

ELEMENTAL ESSENCES

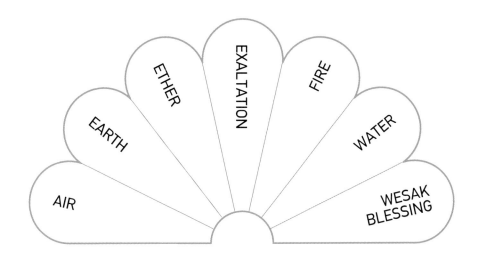

GEM ESSENCES

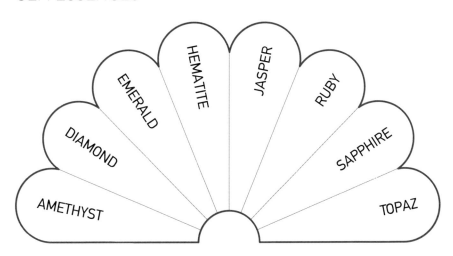

Frequently Asked Questions

THESE FAQS ARE PRETTY MUCH STRAIGHT OFF OUR WEBSITE.

Can I use many essences at the same time?
When combining, it is advisable to choose essences that complement each other (e.g. for anger, resentment and frustration) and that not too many issues are addressed all at once.
Combination formulas, for example Life Force, count as one essence and can be used intermittently alongside a course of essences as and when needed.

What can I expect?
Many people find relief in times of emotional stress, gain insight during periods of transition and experience greater self-awareness. They are also catalysts to personal growth and transformation and ongoing use can help you along your spiritual path. The response may be quick and powerful or may be subtler; a feeling of clarity, peace, or a sense of wellbeing.

How soon will the essences start to make a difference?
Some essences can have an almost immediate effect (the combination formulas in particular), though generally changes are more indistinct as balance and equilibrium are restored in the emotional and subtle bodies. No claims are made that flower essences can cure physical illnesses, yet they often bring improvement to a physical condition.
It depends also on how long you've had the condition. For long-standing, deep-seated issues, we recommend taking the essence for a few weeks and re-evaluating at the end of that period of time. Then either repeat the essences or choose others appropriate for the changed symptom picture.

What happens if I take the wrong essence?
Nothing. You may have chosen the 'wrong' essence. For example, if you took Stonecrop essence to assist you to change and move through a 'block' and there was no effect or it didn't seem to make a difference, it could be because there is no blockage for the essence to dissolve.

Should I stop taking the essences if I feel worse?

It depends. You may be experiencing what is called in homeopathy an "aggravation" or a healing crisis where the condition is temporarily exacerbated. In this case, you can choose to either continue with the course, recognising you are in a process of releasing emotional symptoms (and sometimes physical symptoms) or you can reduce the dosage to once or twice a day only.

If you feel you cannot cope, consider stopping the essence temporarily and use another essence or formula to support you during this time, for example First Aid, Heart Support or Calm Me Down.

Are flower essences safe to use for children and pets?

They are completely natural and safe to use by anyone. Children and pets respond very quickly to flower essences, which may be because they are generally less emotionally 'cluttered' than adults. They can also be used environmentally and for plants and trees.

Is there an alternative to using brandy alcohol in preparing my own dosage bottle?

You can use just pure water but it is best to keep the bottle in the refrigerator. Brandy acts as a preservative and the shelf life is a few years. When prepared with water alone, the shelf life is a few weeks.

Dose bottles can also be prepared using vegetable glycerine. The proportions are one-part vegetable glycerine to one-part water and then add the stock flower essence/s as per usual. Shake the bottle well each time before administering.

You can also prepare a dose by adding a few drops of stock essences to a glass of water and sip throughout the day.

Can I take flower essences with other medicines?

Flower essences work primarily on vibrational levels and more on the subtle bodies and do not interfere with homeopathic, herbal or allopathic treatments. There are no contraindications for them being used alongside any other healing modality, including traditional medicine.

Can I take flower essences during pregnancy?

It is safe to use flower essences during pregnancy. Some midwives administer or recommend them as they offer gentle but efficacious support before, during and after labour. Findhorn Flower Essences offers a few specially prepared formulas: Birthing Essence and Baby Blues Essence, as well as Fertility (pre-pregnancy).

My partner doesn't believe in essences or vibrational medicine. Can I slip some into his tea or coffee?

This is not recommended as he or she might have a healing crisis. Then you would have to own up. It would be to better to introduce essences over time and to show by example that they work.

Essences are not placebos, so you don't have to believe in them for them to work. This is evident when given to children and pets.

Cullerne House nestled within Cullerne Gardens   Buddha in the rockery

Home of Findhorn Flower Essences

Cullerne House

Cullerne House is the home of Findhorn Flower Essences and sits nestled in the midst of the Foundation's organic gardens. Here, fruit and vegetables are grown for the community's dining rooms, tended by staff, volunteers, guests and visitors.

Cullerne Seasons

Winter: earth element

Autumn: water element

Spring: air element

Flower attunement cards

Summer garden borders

Summer: fire element

Child making essence

Gems and Elementals

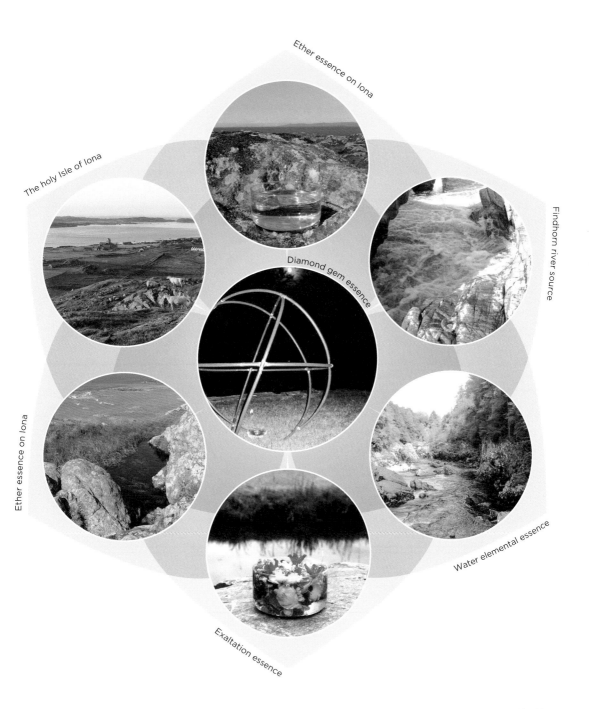

Ether essence on Iona

The holy Isle of Iona

Findhorn river source

Diamond gem essence

Ether essence on Iona

Water elemental essence

Exaltation essence

Universal Hall

Nature Sanctuary

Findhorn Ecovillage

Healing Conference

Cluny Hill

Whiskey Barrel House

Findhorn River

Findhorn Foundation

The Findhorn Foundation is a spiritual community, ecovillage and international centre for holistic learning, helping to unfold a new human consciousness and create a positive and sustainable future.

In 1962, the three co-founders, Eileen and Peter Caddy, their three children, and their friend Dorothy Maclean, towed their caravan to the Findhorn Bay Caravan Park. From these humble beginnings the community has grown in size and complexity and in 2012 celebrates it's 50th birthday with workshops, events and conferences throughout the year.

The founding principles of deep inner listening, co-creation with the intelligence of nature, and service to the world through love in action, have always been at the heart of the community. They remain alive and strong as we stay relevant to the needs of today and evolve into the 21st century.

Eileen, Peter and Dorothy engaged with their inner source of wisdom and the original Findhorn Garden was established through necessity to feed the growing family who were surviving on a low income. The garden flourished and they came to understand they were engaged in a process of co-creation with nature.

Enormous vegetables growing in barren soil drew attention to this remote area of Scotland and inspired others to work in similar ways. This, along with the publication of Eileen's guidance, launched Findhorn onto the world stage and drew visitors from all over the globe.

The educational aspect of the community began under the guidance of David Spangler in the early 70's. Experience Week, an essential Findhorn programme, has so far welcomed over 30,000 people to engage in a heart-opening introduction to the rhythms of community life, including meditation, sharing, sacred dance and being in nature.

Spirituality and ecology are closely linked as people strive to live more consciously. The low carbon pioneering Findhorn Ecovillage at The Park began in the mid 80's and sustainable values are expressed through the innovative use of building materials, the beauty in the architecture and gardens, and applied technology in the Living Machine sewage treatment facility and electricity-generating wind turbines.

Throughout its history the Findhorn Foundation has shared the values of the United Nations, aiming to create a more peaceful and sustainable world. In 1997 the Foundation was approved for formal association with the United Nations, through the Department of Public Information, as a recognised Non-Governmental Organisation.

This cooperation has the potential to be a major vehicle for human evolution, as it supports the process of framing current world issues within a context of global interdependence. Our founders would be proud of how the community has developed and how it continues the commitment of applying timeless wisdom to the challenges of modern day life.

Glossary

AFFIRMATION Mantra or phrase linked to positive thinking, repeated in meditation or said out loud.

ANTAHKARANA Ageless Wisdom term, meaning rainbow bridge, used in connection with the subtle matter, which is built up between the spiritual triad of soul, mind and brain, through meditation practice.

ASTRAL BODY The second human personality body above the dense physical. Also known as the 'Desire Body', it is the subtle or not-so-subtle body where all our emotions and desires are contained.

ALIGNMENT Linear process of linking up vertically the personality bodies to the soul and beyond. Used at the start of a meditation.

ATTUNEMENT The ability or technique to transcend mundane human consciousness. Going beyond dualistic thought to no conscious separation between *deva,* human and other kingdoms of nature. The ability to communicate within these realms.

BODHISATTVA Buddhist term for someone who has developed *bodhicitta,* the aspiration to obtain enlightenment in order to benefit all sentient beings.

CHAKRA/CENTRE The Sanskrit word *chakra* means "wheel". In traditional yoga philosophy, the *chakras* are subtle force centres that vitalise and govern the physical body.

CLEAVAGE In Esoteric Psychology, a cleavage is a separation between one and more of the subtle bodies.

CONSCIOUS MIND The totality of an individual's thoughts, feelings and perceptions.

DEVA From the Sanskrit, it means 'shining one', a being of light or angel. According to Dorothy Maclean, *devas* are archetypal thoughts or energies.

DOCTRINE OF SIGNATURES An age-old herbalists' philosophy that the physical form of a plant, the habitat in which it grows, its taste and scent are indications of what part of the body or which system that herb plant will treat. Paracelsus (1491–1541) developed the concept and published it in his writings.

ETHERIC Subtle electrical field that interpenetrates and vitalises the dense physical body of all living things.

HIGHER SELF True self, represented by the soul or the monad.

HOMEOSTASIS The ability to maintain a relatively constant internal environment; the tendency toward a relatively stable equilibrium between interdependent elements, especially as maintained by physiological processes.

MONAD	The One. The immortal essence of ourselves that uses the soul to incarnate through, just as the soul incarnates through the threefold personality of physical, emotional and mental bodies.
NADI	The subtle matrix that makes up the etheric body. Where many *nadi* cross over each other there is a plexus or *chakra*.
PRANA	Life-giving source stemming from the sun and taken through the root *chakra* and stored in the spleen minor *chakra;* best source of *prana* is near trees and by running water.
PSYCHE	(From the Greek) Soul or Mind.
SHADOW SELF	According to transpersonal psychology, the 'shadow' consists of 'sub-personalities', disowned parts of the self. When incited, they engender unconscious behaviour patterns. One is largely cut off from these patterns, as they operate from the unconscious mind, having been relegated there as coping strategies. A childhood trauma that is repressed is an example, but it doesn't have to be so serious as this.
SOUL	Middle principle, higher self, or "mind" that 'mediates' between the Monad and the lower threefold personality (the synthesis of physical, emotional and mental bodies) on the physical plane.
SUB-CONSCIOUS MIND	is frequently used to mean the "unconscious", which it is not. It is the part of the mind that holds accessible thoughts and memories.
UNCONSCIOUS MIND	is used in psychology to refer to thoughts that are not present in the conscious mind. They are like distant memories that we can't access at our choosing.
UNIVERSAL MIND	The creative vehicle behind everything in existence in the Cosmos; accessible to human beings.
WITNESS	is used for dowsing to represent the client when he or she isn't physically present. The witness allows you to focus on and connect to the person, as if they were physically present. The witness can be a photograph of the client, a sample of hair, or simply a signature.
YOGI	One who has mastered himself and controls his senses.

References

Bach Dr E (1984)
Heal Thyself: An explanation of the real cause and cure of disease, p 30, C.W. Daniel Company Ltd, England

Bach Dr E. (1931)
Ye Suffer from Yourselves by Dr E Bach from lecture given in Southport, 1931

Bailey A. (1922-)
A Treatise on Cosmic Fire, p66 and 667
Letters on Occult Meditation, p183
New York: Lucis Publishing Co.

Emoto M (2005)
The True Power of Water; Beyond Words Publishing Co, USA

Findhorn Community (4th edition; 2008)
The Findhorn Garden Story; p25; Findhorn Press; Scotland

Gurudas (1985)
Gem Elixirs and Vibrational Healing Vol 1. p 2, Cassandra Press, USA

Harvey C and Cochrane A (1995)
The Encyclopaedia of Flower Remedies, p IX, HarperCollins Publishers, London

Steiner R (1979)
Man as Symphony of the Creative Word, p124, p130, Rudolf Steiner Press, London

Stewart C (1939)
Gem Stones of the Seven Rays, pp 9-10, The Theosophical Society, India

The Mother (1992)
Flowers and their Messages, Sri Aurobindo Ashram Press, India

Tansley DV (1977)
Subtle Body: Essence and Shadow, p46, Thames and Hudson Ltd, London

Credits

BAFEP (British Association of Flower Essence Producers) for the FAQ's

Bach Centre (www.bachcentre.com/other/contact.htm)

Cwmhiraeth (2011)
Photo of English stonecrop published on Wikipedia

Ecelan (2009)
Photo of Prunus lusitanica published on Wikipedia

Fischer C (2011)
Photo of *Potentilla anserine* published on Wikipedia

Griffith, R (2009)
Photo of Ragged Robin published on Wikipedia

Howaldt J (2005)
Photo of *Cakile maritime* published on Wikipedia

Sannse (2004)
Photo of Pennywort flower published on Wikipedia

Siegmund, W (2007)
Photo of Bluebell-of-Scotland published on Wikipedia

Tigerente (2005)
Photo of Campanula rotondifolia published on Wikipedia

Velela (2005)
Photo of Hazel flower published on Wikipedia

Bibliography

Akeroyd J (1999)
The Encyclopedia of Wild Flowers; Paragon, Bath

Allen D & Hatfield G (2004)
Medicinal Plants in Folk Tradition; Timber Press, Cambridge

Bailey, Alice A. (1922-)
A Treatise on the Seven Rays Vol. I – V; New York, Lucis Publishing Co.

Barker J (2001)
The Medicinal Flora of Britain and North Western Europe; Winter Press, West Wickham, Kent

Beyerl P (1984)
The Master Book of Herbalism; Phoenix Publishing, Washington

Beyer P (1988)
Herbal Guides A Compendium of Herbal Magick; Phoenix Publishing Inc., U.SA

The British Association of Flower Essence Producers
www.bafep.com

Culpeper N (1995)
Culpeper's Complete Herbal; Wordsworth, Ware

Cunningham S (1995)
Cunningham's Encyclopedia of Magical Herbs; Llewellyn Publications, Minnesota

Cunningham S (2001)
Cunningham's Encyclopedia of Magical Herbs; Llewellyn Publications, Minnesota

Elias T & Dykeman P (1990)
Edible Wild Plants; Sterling Press, England

Findhorn Community (1980)
Faces of Findhorn: Images of a Planetary Family; Harper Collins, England

Gerard J (1998)
Gerard's Herbal; Senate, Twickenham

Gienger M (2005)
Healing Crystals: The A-Z Guide to 430 Gemstones; Earthdancer Books, Scotland

Grieve M (1973)
A Modern Herbal; Merchant; West Molesey

Hoffman D (1996)
The Complete Illustrated Holistic Herbal; Element, Shaftsbury

Hoffman D (1990)
The New Holistic Herbal; Element Books Ltd, United Kingdom

Hopking A (2005)
Esoteric Healing; Blue Dolphin Publishing, USA

Hopman E (1995)
A Druid's Herbal; Destiny Books, Vermont

Kear K (2000)
Flower Wisdom; Thorsons, London

Lavender S & Franklin A (1996)
Herb Craft; Capall Bann, Chieveley.

McIntyre A (1996)
The Complete Floral Healer; Gaia Books, London

Menzies Trull C (2003)
Herbal Medicine; Faculty of Physiomedical Herbal Medicine, Newcastle

Grieve M (1980)
A Modern Herbal; Penguin Books, London

Oken A (1996)
Soul Centred Astrology: A Key to your Expanding Self; The Crossing Press, California

Potterton, D (2002)
Culpeper's Colour Herbal; p 55; Foulsham, London

Steiner, R (1979)
Man as Symphony of the Creative Word; Rudolf Steiner Press, London

Steiner, R (1983)
Fundamentals of Therapy; Rudolf Steiner Press, England

Tansley DV (1988)
Chakras Rays and Radionics; C.W. Daniel Co Ltd, England

Please contact us for further information
on products or workshops

FINDHORN
FLOWER
ESSENCES

Cullerne House
Findhorn
Morayshire
Scotland
IV36 3YY

Telephone
+44 (1309) 690129

Email
info@findhornessences.com

Website
www.findhornessences.com

Facebook
Findhorn Flower Essences